A BURDEN OF SILENCE

My Mother's Battle with AIDS

By

Nancy A. Draper

authorHOUSE

1663 LIBERTY DRIVE, SUITE 200
BLOOMINGTON, INDIANA 47403
(800) 839-8640
www.authorhouse.com

First published by AuthorHouse 07/07/04

ISBN: 1-4184-5106-1 (e)
ISBN: 1-4184-5107-X (sc)

Library of Congress Control Number: 2004106828

Printed in the United States of America
Bloomington, Indiana

This book is printed on acid-free paper.

*The names of the people mentioned in

A BURDEN OF SILENCE: My Mother's Battle with AIDS

are fictitious, except for

Dr. Ann Webster, Ph.D., and Betty, my mother's hospice nurse.

Acknowledgments

I am thankful to those individuals who encouraged and supported me in writing this book. Their support, assistance, and suggestions in making this book a reality are greatly appreciated. Among the people who did so are in alphabetical order: Maureen Hastings, Ruth Johnson, Susan Paluska, Nina Peterson, Ann Pozen, Psy.D., Erin Robinson, Maggie Sund, Ph.D., Joyce Szczapa, and Ann Webster, Ph.D.

Special thanks to Avon Books and the NAMES Project Foundation.

I send a special thought to my deceased mother; for this is her story.

Dedication

This book is dedicated to

My husband, Floyd, whose love and support comforted me during difficult times.

My two sons, Tom and Shawn, whose encouragement helped me write this book.

All AIDS patients everywhere, and their caretakers.

All hospice workers who provide love, support, and compassion.

And especially in memory of my mother, who suffered in silence. Through this book, her voice will finally be heard.

I wish she were here.

Table of Contents

~ 1 ~

"No One Must Find Out"

"This has to remain a secret, Nancy," my father whispers as he sits in our pine rocking chair with a somber expression on his face. My inner voice tells me he is about to reveal ominous news. I have just come home from my yoga class and was surprised to see Dad's car in our driveway so late in the evening. I am worried about my mother.

"What secret, Dad? Why are you here alone? Is Mom okay?" I ask nervously.

Mom had been released from the hospital three weeks ago with no concrete diagnosis from her doctors. They were baffled by her condition. For the past few years she had been suffering with fevers, night sweats, swollen glands, and a lingering cough. I suspect his news relates to her health.

Obviously distressed, he looks at my husband, Floyd and me as we sit on the couch waiting for him to reveal this secret.

"I'm sorry to visit so late, but Mom and I have been stressed all week waiting for the results of a blood test."

"What kind of blood test?"

"Last Monday, Dr. Willet asked Mom's permission to have her blood tested for HIV infection."

"What? Why would he want her tested for HIV infection?"

"After examining her medical records, he discovered Mom was transfused with four units of blood during her heart bypass surgery. They were traced to New York City where AIDS is becoming a raging epidemic. Dr. Willet is suspicious that she might have been infected with contaminated blood," he explains as Floyd holds my hand in support. "He's checking into it now. Mom and I were both hesitant to tell you sooner because we didn't want you to worry," he said, his voice quivering. "Mom was scared to take the HIV test, but she knew it was necessary to determine if she is HIV infected."

I feel like a sledge hammer is slamming against my chest. Stunned by Dad's words, I sip a drink of juice from the glass Floyd brings me to help calm me. As Dad continues to talk, I attempt to mask my fear. My throat is tense and my heart is racing as if I were running a marathon. I have to remain calm. I can't upset Dad. He is grief-stricken and worried about the test results. If she is infected, he could be carrying the deadly virus himself. I'm sure he has already thought of that possibility.

"When will they notify her of the test results?" I ask anxiously.

"The doctor's office should be calling any day now. We just sit by the phone and wait," Dad replies as he continues to lean toward us, talking quietly, not wanting his grandsons who were upstairs to hear our conversation.

"Mom isn't taking this very well, Nancy," Dad says, clearly dazed and exhausted.

"Dr. Willet said it would take at least another week before we know for certain. If the ELISA test proves positive, they'll perform the Western Blot test to confirm the diagnosis."

The possibility that Mom could have been infected with HIV contaminated blood during her heart bypass operation in 1983 was horrifying. A sense of rage permeated my body. People who had been diagnosed as HIV eventually died from AIDS when their immune system could no longer fight off infections.

It had been five years since Mom had her surgery. Now, in September of 1988, doctors were questioning whether the blood she had received was infected with HIV.

"I don't understand. I thought the blood banks were supposed to notify an individual if they might have been infected through a blood transfusion."

Dad just shakes his head in frustration replying, "I really don't know."

If the blood bank was concerned that a person had received contaminated blood, I thought it was their responsibility to notify the recipient. Then the person could be tested for HIV infection. But no one had contacted Mom.

"Then maybe there's a chance she isn't infected," I say to Dad.

But could the blood bank have known and not informed her?

It is late at night. Shocked by Dad's news, I sit on the couch in disbelief. I imagine how distressing it is for her to have to wait so long for the results of a test to determine whether she has a terminal illness.

Why hadn't the doctors paid more attention to her symptoms? Could it be because she is a sixty-six year old grandmother and not in a high risk category for contracting AIDS?

Dad looks at both of us intently and whispers, "I want you to understand that if the test results come back HIV-positive, we have decided to keep this a secret. No one must find out. We don't want the grandchildren to know about this. Mom and I are afraid of what people might think or do. People might reject us if they know that Mom is infected with HIV. We just can't take any chances." His voice is raspy and he is exhausted. "We're too old to fight any discrimination."

"If she's been infected with HIV it isn't her fault. Just remember that the test could prove negative. But if the test results prove she is infected, we'll find a way to deal with it," I say reassuringly.

Dad doesn't respond. He is confused and shaken. Everything is happening so quickly. As he gets up from his chair to walk over to us he says, "Well, I promised Mom I wouldn't stay too long. Every day she paces the house worrying that she is infected. She's very depressed and cries most of the time."

I give Dad a hug and say, "Please try not to worry."

"I'll let you know as soon as we hear anything," he says as he walks alone into the dark, rainy September evening.

After Dad leaves the house, Floyd holds me in his arms. I can't believe that two hours ago I had been in my yoga class where the scent of sandalwood and the soothing nature music led me to a state of deep relaxation. That peace is now replaced with fear and concern about Mom's health. I attempt to use the deep breathing exercises I learned this evening to relieve the tension. I begin to feel more relaxed for a few minutes, but the anxiety concerning the test results is a constant companion.

* * *

I woke up the next morning exhausted and completely overwhelmed at the thought Mom could be dying. I decided to visit with her that afternoon to offer my support. Even though there were no magical words I could possibly say to ease her anxiety and depression, I could at least offer her companionship and support while she waited for the final test results.

Driving to her house, I realized my mind was wandering. A quick glance at my speedometer indicated I was exceeding the speed limit. I saw blue, flashing police lights in my rear view mirror. *Oh no! I don't need this now.* I pulled over and rolled down the car window to speak to the police officer, wiping tears from my eyes.

"Are you all right, Miss? I saw you swerving down the hill."

"Yes, Officer," I replied. "I'm going to visit my sick mother. I guess I was driving a little too fast." He must have felt sympathy, as he allowed me to go with a warning.

"Maybe you should just concentrate on your driving and slow down a bit," he reprimanded me gently.

If he only knew the emotional tightrope I was walking.

As I entered my parents' driveway, I convinced myself that I must be strong for both of them. Hopefully, God would give me supportive words to ease Mom's anxiety.

I knocked on the front door and within seconds Mom came to greet me with a warm hug; tears streaming down her cheeks. Her sallow face reflected her weariness and lack of sleep. Her eyes were bloodshot from several days of crying. I embraced her…trying to offer some solace. Hopefully, in another week we would know the final results and be relieved from this panic we were all experiencing. It will have been just a ghastly nightmare.

As I held her, I spoke softly. "It's okay, Mom," trying to provide some peace and hope. Secretly, I felt helpless.

But then I had an idea. For the past three weeks, I had been taking reflexology classes learning how to massage the feet to benefit different areas of the body. Some people believe reflexology has a healing effect on the immune system. In any case, Mom always enjoyed having her feet massaged.

"Mom, how would you like a foot massage today?" I asked with a smile, hoping she would agree to my offer.

"Are you sure you want to touch me?" she asked. "I might be *dirty* with the AIDS virus."

"Mom, you are not *dirty* and please don't think of yourself that way. We don't know the test results yet. There's still a good chance that the blood was safe, and you will not come down with HIV infection." She nodded her head consenting to the massage.

"You just sit down in the lounge chair and relax."

Tears began to trickle down her cheek as I massaged her feet. Her large brown eyes, red and swollen, were riveted on my face.

"Nancy," she whispered, "you're so nice to do this for me. I love you." She placed her hand on my shoulder. "I don't want you to worry about me. You have your own health problems."

"Don't you start worrying about me, Mom. I'm fine."

After I finished massaging Mom's feet, I suggested, "Why don't you read an intriguing mystery novel? Maybe that will help take your mind off this awful waiting period." She was an avid reader and a frequent visitor to the public library; however, I knew it would be difficult for her to concentrate.

As I left the house, I reached out to give her another hug. She held on as if she didn't want me to leave. I looked at my watch and realized that it was getting late.

"I have to go now. Several students are coming to the house for their piano lessons this afternoon. I wish I could stay longer."

"Thank you for coming today, Nancy. It really helped me feel better," she said as I slowly walked down her front steps admiring her spectacular flower garden. Her neighbors marveled at her stunning, colorful garden and how she had designed it so creatively. She always found peace in planting her flower bed each spring. Geraniums, marigolds, begonias, and petunias were among her favorite flowers, and she had created borders of them around the house. Now, in a weakened state, she was unable to really enjoy her favorite hobby.

"I'll call you tomorrow," I said as I walked toward my car. Once inside, I rolled down the window and blew her a kiss. She lifted her hand and blew one back at me as I drove away.

During my ride home, I remembered how Dad had questioned the surgeon and cardiologist about having his friends from the Lions Club donate blood for Mom in case she required a blood transfusion. Since we were aware of the risk of AIDS from listening to the news on television, we didn't want to take a chance that the blood she received would be contaminated. The cardiologist and surgeon had assured Dad that the blood supply was safe and that it would not be necessary to use designated donors for the surgery. Obviously, the doctors didn't realize the need to take precautions to protect Mom from contaminated blood. They didn't recommend designated blood donors since they had blood stored in their own hospital.

The fact that there was no blood screening for HIV-positive blood in January of 1983 deeply concerned me. Newspapers and television newscasters had reported cases of HIV infection and AIDS deaths throughout the United States...especially in New York City, Los Angeles, and San Francisco. These included homosexuals, hemophiliacs, intravenous drug users, babies of mothers who were infected with the virus and babies who had received transfusions at birth. It was known in January of 1983, before my mother's surgery, that AIDS was a blood-borne disease.

How I wished we had been more assertive and insisted that the doctors agreed to use blood donated from our friends. Maybe we could have escaped this nightmare.

The following Monday evening I attended my yoga class searching for some peace of mind. For the past few days, I had been unable to sleep more than three hours a night. Each morning when I awoke, reality set in. The realization that Mom could be HIV-positive consumed every waking moment. Waiting for the test results was unbearable.

My God! What will we do if the HIV test proves positive? I had to stop this unhealthy, negative thinking.

During the entire yoga class, I attempted to follow the relaxation instructions. I found it difficult to meditate at the end of the class. My mind raced frantically, unable to focus on the peaceful prayer mantra I had chosen.

"Are you all right tonight?" my instructor asked as I was leaving class.

Since I couldn't reveal our family secret, I replied, "Yes, my mind is just occupied tonight with other issues. I'll be fine."

Outside, the brisk autumn air and colorful falling leaves temporarily took my mind off my apprehension and fear as I drove home. The soft jazz station I was listening to provided a respite from the frightening thoughts running through my mind.

When I walked into the house, Floyd was standing by the kitchen counter. His expression told me the news was not good.

"Sit down for a minute, Nancy," he said gently. "Your father called tonight with the results of the HIV test. Mom tested positive for HIV infection." His voice was restrained as he tried to hold back his own sorrow.

I felt numb…paralyzed by the fear. This was *real!* No more wondering… no more hope. The death verdict had been given to my mother over the phone. It was too late in the evening to call her. Besides, in my state of mind, I didn't know if I could provide an ounce of support. I desperately needed someone to hold and comfort me since I was so angry and frightened. As Floyd held me, my whole body shook uncontrollably.

Tom and Shawn were upstairs finishing their homework. They had no idea what we had been dealing with. I didn't want this burden to affect them and their school work, so we had to keep silent about Mom's illness. In any case, Dad had asked us to keep it a secret from them. I didn't know how long I could manage that since we had always shared our sorrows and concerns with each other.

Tom came downstairs to ask me a question concerning his homework assignment. I tried to pull myself together. I was battling anger and fear as I attempted to calmly answer Tom's question. After he went back upstairs, I panicked. My body was trembling and my heart was pounding.

"I have to get out of here NOW!" I cried to Floyd.

"Where are you going?" Floyd asked, distressed.

"I don't know…I don't care. I just need to SCREAM! I can't stay here and whisper."

I looked at the glass in my hand. How I wanted to smash that glass into the kitchen door. I had never felt so much fear and rage! I grabbed the coat I had thrown on the chair after my yoga class and dashed to the front door.

"Wait a minute, Nancy, I'll go with you. I don't want you out alone in your emotional state." We sat in the car until I stopped crying for a minute to catch my breath and speak. "Where do you want to go?" he asked sympathetically.

"I don't care...I don't know," I yelled. "Just take me away from this house so I can scream!" As he backed out of the driveway, I began to cry out, "Nooo, Nooo this can't be happening. Please, God...not my precious mother." I rocked back and forth in the car crying, "No, please, no!"

Floyd drove me to the empty church parking lot. Feeling weak and shaky, I managed to get out of the car and started kicking dirt and stones on the pavement. "It just can't be! How could this have happened? Why? Why?" I exclaimed to Floyd. I couldn't lose my mother to such a vicious disease. She still had so much to live for.

I walked to the statue of Mary in front of the church and cried, "Why my mother? This isn't fair!" I shouted. We stayed there for about thirty minutes. Floyd attempted to console me but I was in shock. My mother was a wonderful lady. She had contracted HIV during a surgical procedure to relieve her angina pains and blocked arteries. This surgery was intended to increase her life span. Instead of helping her live a better and longer life, she would die an agonizing death from AIDS. Her hope of living to see her grandchildren grow to adulthood vanished with Dr. Willet's phone call. She was going to be fighting a battle she knew she couldn't win. The drugs given to combat it were almost as bad as the disease itself. Somehow, I had to find a way to console her and help her cope.

We went back home. I couldn't sleep all night wondering how we would survive this tragedy. Pretending everything was fine in front of Tom and Shawn was stressful. I hated lying to them. Since I didn't talk too much about my mother in front of them, they didn't ask many questions. They had their school work to do and I didn't want to have them focused on the heartbreak we were living with.

Lord, don't we have enough problems? I had never complained before concerning the medical problems we were coping with. At the age of twenty-nine, three months after Shawn's birth, I was diagnosed with rheumatoid arthritis and two weeks later with polymyositis, a serious muscle disease that caused pain and inflammation in my muscles. I could barely walk or climb stairs. Since my hands were swollen and stiff from the rheumatoid arthritis, preparing Shawn's bottles was an arduous task. I became frustrated as they would often slip out of my hands onto the floor.

A year later, Shawn was diagnosed with quadriplegic cerebral palsy at the age of fifteen months. I had difficulty taking care of my two sons when my joints and muscles were extremely painful and weak.

Tom had his own battle with dyslexia that required him to work on his homework late into the night. Unfortunately, his *hidden* handicap was not fully understood by many teachers. Being a teacher, I was able to provide him with extra help. His persistence to do well always managed to list him on the honor roll. Now, my own mother was fighting the dreaded AIDS virus. *How could I possibly handle this?*

I knew I had to be pro-active and discover ways to help my mother cope with this deadly virus. Our deep faith had always brought us through our tribulations. I prayed somehow we would have the strength to cope with this new devastating tragedy in our lives.

~ 2 ~

Death Verdict

I was furious that the doctor had delivered the bad news over the telephone. No counseling…just the *death verdict.* Dad called me the next morning to tell me that Mom overheard the questions he asked Dr. Willet. "Nancy, Mom was so nervous when she heard me talking to Dr. Willet. I asked him if he was certain that the test results were positive for HIV-infection. Mom became hysterical when she heard that question."

"What does Dr. Willet suggest Mom do now?" I asked.

"He suggested calling his office in the morning to speak to his secretary to schedule an appointment. I called this morning and was able to schedule an appointment this Friday."

"Well, that's only three days away, Dad. At least Mom will be able to ask Dr. Willet questions on what she can do to fight this virus. I would like to go to the appointment with you on Friday." I was more knowledgeable about the virus than Mom and Dad and more assertive in asking questions pertaining to her treatment. I felt confident I could provide support and be my mother's advocate in dealing with this devastating diagnosis. I was also aware that some doctors take advantage of older people and often rush them out of the office. I couldn't let that happen to my mother. There were too many questions to be answered.

"Yes, Nancy, I would like you to come with us. Thank you," Dad said gratefully.

On Friday, we arrived at the clinic a few minutes early. Mom always took pride in being punctual. She looked like a perfect lady dressed in her tailored beige suit with matching shoes and pocketbook. As we walked into the hospital lobby, she reached out to hold my hand and cried, "I feel dizzy, Nancy. Help me!" She was having difficulty breathing and was hyperventilating.

Thinking she might faint, I suggested, "Sit down in this chair. Try to do some of the breathing techniques I taught you at home."

"Nancy, I can't concentrate on my breathing now," she cried in panic. She was beyond my help. Mom was desperate, frightened, and confused by this horrific diagnosis. I had to take charge. There was no time to concentrate on my fears.

I remembered how several years ago, I would never have been able to handle this situation due to a panic disorder that led to agoraphobia. The panic disorder started my junior year in college and lasted for seventeen years. I wasn't able to attend many functions for fear of fainting and having an anxiety attack. I would often have to "white-knuckle" it through necessary functions I had to attend such as weddings and dinner events. Going to the movies or to a restaurant usually brought immense anxiety. However, with the use of behavioral techniques, including visualization, deep breathing exercises, and cognitive thinking, I had recovered enough to deal with this new crisis in our family.

Eventually, Mom began to feel more in control and we walked down the hospital corridor to the doctor's office. After sitting thirty minutes in the waiting room of the infectious disease department, the nurse called my mother's name. She led us into a small examining room. Dr. Willet walked in after us and sat across from Mom with the voluminous medical chart resting on his lap.

After greeting us, he directed his attention to Mom as he mumbled, "As I told your husband over the telephone, you have tested HIV-positive. You received four units of blood during your heart bypass surgery in 1983. You contracted the HIV infection from the blood transfusion you were given during the operation. We discovered one of the donors was HIV-positive." He spoke softly. Mom was straining to hear every word he uttered.

My mother's expression was anxious as she leaned toward him to hear his explanation. Realizing she was not comprehending what he was saying, I said, "Dr. Willet, my mother can't hear very well, especially when she is nervous and frightened. Could you please speak a little louder?"

He nodded his head. "One donor you received blood from was HIV-positive," he reiterated. "That's the reason you have been sick with flu-like symptoms, the frequent fevers, fatigue, and swollen lymph nodes. You have been infected for the past five years."

Mom was so confused and petrified; she couldn't focus on his words or think of what to say. He continued speaking, but didn't really offer any suggestions as to what she should do now to relieve her deteriorating physical condition and severe depression.

She kept leaning closer to his chair attempting to understand his every word. Even though she was an intelligent woman, she had no knowledge of HIV or AIDS and was not able to ask many questions. Scared and confused, Mom asked, her voice strained, "Doctor, if this happened to *your* wife, what would you do?"

He looked down for a moment and responded sheepishly, "I really don't know what I would do."

"Well, what can *I* do now?" she asked, frustrated.

"I'm afraid there's not much that can be done to help you. As you realize, there is no cure for HIV infection. It eventually leads to full-blown AIDS."

"Where would you direct my mother for help?" I questioned. "There must be something she can do."

"Unfortunately, there's really nothing we can do except monitor her condition," he replied. Looking at Mom, he suggested, "It might be wise to have your T-cell count checked. I'll send you to the lab to get some blood work done." He continued to explain to us that if the T-cell count is low or below 200 she would be more prone to suffer from certain opportunistic infections, such as the cytomegalovirus or CMV that attacks the brain or other organs of the body. He went on to explain about the dangers of *Pneumocystis carinii* pneumonia or often called PCP. Dr. Willet said that this was a rare type of pneumonia usually found in AIDS patients who have an impaired immune system.

"I don't know anymore to tell you," he replied. He stood up and began to usher us out of his pristine office. He had spent a mere fifteen minutes with us. To me, that didn't seem enough time to spend with a woman who had just been given a death sentence.

"Wait a minute, Dr. Willet," I said assertively, "I have some more questions."

He stood by the door as I asked, "Do you think my mother would benefit from psychoneuroimmunology? I know that the mind/body connection is a powerful tool in healing the immune system."

He gave me a blank stare and replied, "Well, I honestly don't feel that it is scientific or will benefit your mother…but you can try whatever you want," he answered. "As I told you, I don't have any answers or advice to give you."

I stared at Mom…grief-stricken and petrified. She was in total shock and disbelief.

As he walked us out of the office, I grabbed his white jacked and said, "Listen to me…a doctor doesn't just tell a patient she is infected with HIV which will likely lead to AIDS and death and then let her walk out the door and fend for herself! She needs to be given some type of support or direction."

"I'm afraid you're right," he admitted. "I feel helpless. I don't have any answers and don't really know what suggestions I can give to you and your parents."

How could a doctor give a death verdict and then not suggest some type of continuing support? Anger began to well up inside. I had to keep in control and remain strong …or at least pretend to. Little did I realize at the time, that the *pretending* was going to rule my life for the next several years.

We sat for a moment. I watched Dad as he attempted to console Mom. Filled with tears, she appeared so innocent and helpless, like a little child. "Nancy, I feel like a leper!" she cried as she put her head on my shoulder.

"Mom, stop…you're not a leper. We will find a way to deal with this." It was heartbreaking for me to have her think of herself as being contaminated.

"Why don't you and Dad go to the lab and get that blood work completed? I will be right back," I promised as I gave her a hug.

I didn't reveal where I was going, but I realized my mother needed some counseling. I immediately headed for the psychiatric department at the other end of the hospital. My mother was in a severe state of depression and needed intensive counseling and support. Finding my way through the maze of hospital corridors was an arduous task. My legs felt like jelly as I attempted to follow the directions to the psychiatry department. I knew I had to be back at the waiting room where they would be meeting me shortly. There wasn't much time to schedule an appointment…but I felt it was necessary. I prayed she could be seen by a doctor as soon as possible.

Finally, after fifteen minutes of racing through the hospital corridors asking for directions, I saw the sign for the psychiatric unit. As I walked over to the desk, I tried to pull myself together to explain the situation clearly. I told the receptionist my mother needed an appointment *ASAP*! When the secretary saw my distress, she replied, "Come follow me." She led me to one of the nurses in charge of booking appointments.

"Thank you for taking the time to speak with me," I said breathlessly. She sat me down and I began to explain the tragedy we were facing. "My sixty-six-year old mother was just diagnosed as HIV-positive four days ago and she is in sheer shock and depression. She really needs to be seen by a psychiatrist as soon as possible," I pleaded. "She can't sleep or eat and cries most of the day."

Seeing my desperation, her eyes filled with tears. "I'm so sorry," she replied. "You stay here for a few minutes and I will see what I can do to help you."

She left the room and within a few minutes returned handing me an appointment card. "I was able to schedule an appointment tomorrow afternoon with Dr. Sanders," she said. "I hope this will help you and your mother."

"Thank you so much," I replied as I squeezed her hand. I knew Mom's blood work would be completed by now, so I dashed back to the waiting room. After all, they had no idea where I had gone. I found both Mom and Dad sitting in the infectious disease waiting room with a look of fear and desperation on their faces.

"Where did you go, Nancy?" Mom asked with curiosity.

When I explained to Mom that I had scheduled an appointment for her tomorrow with a psychiatrist, she was not very receptive to the idea. Being a very private person, she didn't think she would feel comfortable sharing her intimate concerns with a doctor she didn't know. She kept most of her feelings inside instead of reaching out for support and help. Besides, this was a big secret. After some persistent persuasion from me, she finally acquiesced. At least the psychiatrist would be able to prescribe some type of medication to alleviate her insomnia and depression.

She didn't say much as we walked to the car. It was obvious she was still numb from her appointment with Dr. Willet. Just before we got into the car, Mom said to Dad, "I'm going to sit in the back seat with Nancy."

On the way home, she held my hand as she looked sadly and intently at me. How hard I tried to control the flood of tears I was holding inside. I had to be strong and find ways to help Mom cope with this ugly illness.

Dad stopped to pick up some groceries on the way home. My mother and I sat alone in the back seat of the car still holding hands.

"Nancy, I want you to understand something. I am going to fight this illness. But I'm so tired…I just don't know if I can win this battle. Please understand," she pleaded.

I nodded my head. Poor Mom…she had been fighting some type of illness most of her life. At the age of thirty-two, she was diagnosed with lymphoma after being told by several doctors that there was nothing wrong with her. They considered her a hypochondriac and made her feel it was all in her head. Her doctor said, "Those swollen lymph glands in your pretty neck are really nothing for you to be concerned about."

Although only six years old, I remember her getting weaker each day. Finally, after several months of being bedridden, she had an appointment at a prestigious hospital in Boston. She was examined by a cancer specialist. He diagnosed Mom with lymphoma and scheduled surgery the next day.

There was constant whispering in our house. My grandparents lived on the other side of our duplex house. Many days I was worried, afraid of what was happening to Mom. Since my parents spoke some French, I would frequently hear French conversations between my parents and grandparents. I was frightened…wondering what they were discussing. The only other time they spoke French in my presence was at Christmas when they wanted to keep secrets about the gifts they were buying. No one told me anything. I missed many days of school due to my constant headaches and stomach pain.

Now we were dealing with secrecy again. Floyd and I had to whisper so our two sons could not overhear our conversations. I felt bad about keeping Mom's illness from them, but I was respecting my parents' wishes.

I thought back to my childhood days and remembered the times my mother would call me into her bedroom so she could give me a bag of gifts. "Nancy, I am going to the hospital for a few days, and I bought these toys for you," she would say. Fear prevented me from asking her why she had to go to the hospital. I was trying to be a "good girl" and not cause my parents to feel uncomfortable. Yet, everyday I worried about my mother and why she had to go to the hospital so often. My grandmother would wait by the phone just in case my father or the doctor called.

"Go out and play, Nancy," Nana would say. "Everything will be fine." Even though I was very young, I could sense the tension in my grandmother's voice and I worried about my mother.

Not until I was seriously ill myself, did I discover from my aunt that Mom had been battling recurrent lymphoma all those years. Those "swollen glands" in her neck were malignant tumors in her lymph nodes that most of her doctors had neglected to diagnose. She was stricken with lymphoma and didn't want to worry me. At twenty-nine, I found myself fighting my own life-threatening disease and taking care of two young sons.

The habit of keeping silent about an illness was now continuing. Mom and Dad were frightened to tell people she was HIV-positive. They thought it was a disgrace and felt certain she would be ostracized if people discovered her condition. But I knew she had to confide in someone. Speaking with a psychologist would allow her to share her anxiety.

The next morning, Dad and Mom picked me up early so we could beat the traffic going into Boston. As I sat in the backseat of the car, I began to be concerned that Dr. Sanders might not have empathy and understanding of her condition. "How many patients with HIV had he counseled… one, ten, or possibly none?" I wondered.

"I'm not sure I want to do this, Nancy," Mom said as we sat together in the waiting room.

"Mom, you can talk to Dr. Sanders about your feelings. He can also help you with your insomnia," I added, hoping she would continue to stay.

A few minutes later my mother's name was called. She walked slowly and with apprehension toward his office. Dad and I sat and waited, hoping and praying this was the right decision for her. A half-hour later, we were called into Dr. Sander's office. He introduced himself and explained how he planned to treat Mom's depression and anxiety.

"I've prescribed a mild tranquilizer for your wife to alleviate her insomnia," he said. "She is certainly under severe stress due to her recent HIV diagnosis."

"Dr. Sanders, have you ever counseled anyone with HIV or AIDS?" I asked.

"No, I have never had an HIV-positive patient," he responded.

Immediately, I became concerned about his ability to counsel my mother concerning her feelings of fear and shame due to her HIV-positive status. He had no experience in working with people with this devastating disease. But at least he was someone to whom she could confide her secret to without anyone discovering her illness. This was a safe haven where she could release her deep fears and emotions.

On the way out, the secretary made a follow-up appointment for Mom the following week to determine if the medication was effective. The doctor had prescribed Ativan which would help her sleep and reduce some of the anxiety.

As we walked down the hospital corridor, I suggested, "Mom, why don't we go up to the gynecology department?"

"Why do you want to go up there, Nancy? I'm really tired and don't feel well. I just want to go home to bed."

"Mom, I think it would be helpful to visit Dr. Jackson. You know how much she cares for you. I'm sure she would want to be aware of your diagnosis."

Dr. Jackson had recently given Mom a gynecological exam and was also baffled by her symptoms. "Yes, I guess I would like to talk to her. But she is probably busy with patients," she replied.

"Well, the only way we'll find out is to go up to her office."

When we arrived at her office, we noticed her standing by her doorway. She saw my mother and gave her a big hug. "It's so nice to see you, Irene. How have you been feeling?" she asked with sincere concern.

Mom started to cry and Dr. Jackson took us into her office. Stumbling over the words, she said, "I was diagnosed a few days ago as HIV-positive."

Dr. Jackson embraced her and tried to comfort her. "Oh, Irene, I am so very sorry." Since Mom was unable to control her tears, Dad and I explained the details of the blood transfusion…the fear she had been going through the past two weeks waiting for the test results…and now her trying to cope with HIV infection.

With tears trickling down her cheeks, Mom looked at Dr. Jackson and asked, "Aren't you afraid to hold me?"

"Irene, please don't think you are contagious. There's no way you can pass your HIV infection to me by hugging," she tried to convince Mom. But Mom couldn't help but feel dirty.

After we discussed her condition for a few more moments, I asked, "Dr. Jackson, do you think my mother could benefit from psychoneuroimmunology?"

Without hesitation, she quickly responded. "Yes, I certainly do. There is a wonderful woman psychologist in charge of support groups for women with HIV/AIDS and cancer at the Deaconess Hospital. Her name is Dr. Ann Webster and she conducts support groups in the Mind/Body Clinic with patients fighting these life threatening illnesses."

I stared at Mom to get her reaction from Dr. Jackson's suggestion. She didn't seem to show any interest in a support group. She found it difficult to share her emotions with other people. However, I had a feeling this would be a perfect place for Mom to receive support and acceptance from other women who were going through the same illness and were probably as frightened as she was now.

After we left Dr. Jackson's office, we headed for the car. Mom was still weak and unsteady on her feet. I decided I would call Dr. Webster the next morning to inquire about these support groups. I had faith I would be successful in convincing Mom to make an appointment with Dr. Webster who was experienced in working with people with HIV and AIDS.

The following morning I called Dr. Webster's office and left a message on her answering machine. I received a phone call from her later in the afternoon. After I explained how Mom had become infected with HIV from a blood transfusion, she was very empathetic to her situation. She proceeded to inform me as to how she conducted her support groups.

"I'm not certain my mother would want to be in a group setting," I answered. "She is so frightened of sharing her feelings. Being infected with HIV has made her feel ashamed and dirty. But I'll give her this information and hopefully she will make an appointment to see you."

A few minutes later, I called Mom on the telephone to discuss the program with her. She was not receptive to being in a group.

"What if someone finds out I'm going there?"

"Please, Mom, stop thinking the worst. Just give it some consideration and we'll discuss it later."

The next day I called Dr. Webster back and told her Mom wasn't being very cooperative and was reluctant to join a group.

"Nancy, I could possibly see her in a private session if she agrees to that," she offered.

"I'll do the best I can to get her into your office to meet with you."

When I approached Mom with the idea, she seemed more willing, but not yet ready to commit to making an appointment. How desperately she needed someone familiar with HIV and AIDS to comfort and calm her fears. I prayed that eventually she would agree to meeting with Dr. Webster…but it would have to be when she was ready.

~ 3 ~

Holistic Coping Skills

A couple of weeks went by and Mom had an appointment with her cardiologist. He was not the doctor Mom had during her heart bypass surgery.

"I don't know why we have to see Dr. Larkin," Mom said. "During my last visit with him he didn't even let me ask any questions. He kept interrupting me when I started to ask him something."

My father was with her but didn't want to upset the doctor. During this visit, I was ready to handle any insensitivity from this cardiologist. I brought a list of questions I wanted answered. I was furious that during Mom's last visit with Dr. Larkin he had failed to give her his full attention by not answering her questions. When we walked into his office, he was sitting at his desk and didn't even bother to get up and greet us. After we said hello to him, he asked his secretary to bring him the results of the latest testing done on Mom.

He looked through them and began scotch taping my mother's reports in her chart. Mom asked him a question and he barked, "Hold on, I can't do two things at the same time."

Poor Mom. She hung her head as if she had done something wrong.

"Dr. Larkin," I said firmly, "I think you can answer a couple of questions while you're doing that." He didn't even respond to my remark. I had never seen a doctor use scotch tape to put information into a medical record.

Frustrated by his actions, I asked, "Listen, may we ask you a few questions now or are you still busy taping?" It seemed he really didn't care about us and had an apathetic expression on his face. Here we were hurting and anxious to have questions answered, and he appeared unconcerned about Mom's emotional or physical condition.

Finally, Mom was able to discuss some matters with him. He was curt with his answers; but at least she received a reply.

As he looked through the record he asked, "Do you have any idea why your surgeon used your leg vein for the heart bypass surgery?"

"They really didn't discuss too much with me," she replied. "I thought they knew best, so I didn't question their decision."

"Well, most of the medical literature pertaining to heart bypass surgery on women suggests using the mammary artery," he explained.

I was upset because I had read a book about heart bypass surgery and read about the benefits of using a woman's mammary artery instead of her leg vein. A woman's mammary artery was larger than a leg vein, and lessened the chance of increased blockage. A man's leg vein was usually larger than a woman's leg vein. Therefore, it was more reasonable to take the woman's mammary artery instead of her leg vein. However, I didn't intervene in the decisions the doctors made concerning her surgery. Instead,

28

we all trusted the doctor's decision. Now, I was angry at myself for not being more assertive and pro-active in Mom's surgery.

"If your cardiologist had taken your mammary artery, you might not have the blockage you currently have. Your test results indicate your arteries started to block within six months after the operation. No wonder you had angina pains so soon after surgery," he explained.

Did it really matter now? I thought to myself. She was infected with HIV positive blood and the doctors seemed to have made wrong decisions by using the leg vein and giving her blood from anonymous donors.

Dr. Larkin gave a prescription to Mom as we were leaving the office. He decided to change her medication since it wasn't agreeing with her. It was lunch time and we decided to eat in the hospital cafeteria. We sat there perplexed, not knowing where to turn next. I saw the desperation in Mom's eyes.

"Mom, why don't we try to see Dr. Webster today?" I realized the chances of seeing her were slim, but we were desperate and needed all the help we could get.

"But we don't have an appointment, Nancy," she replied.

I knew that if I could get her over to the Deaconess Hospital, then we would at least have a chance of meeting with Dr. Webster. Mom agreed and we went into the Mind/Body Clinic to see if she was in. We walked into the office and I asked the secretary if we could see Dr. Webster.

"I'm sorry, but she's in a conference meeting right now," she responded.

I took a pen and piece of note paper out of my pocket and began writing a note to Dr. Webster. I handed it to the secretary and said, "Is it possible for you to bring this message to her?"

Within five minutes, the secretary came out of the meeting room and said, "Dr. Webster said she will take a short break from the meeting so she can visit with you."

Thank you, Lord! I thought to myself. I knew from my phone conversations with her that she was a caring person who would go out of her way to help. I sat next to Mom while we waited. I knew she was a little frightened. Within five minutes, a slim, attractive woman started walking toward us.

"You must be Nancy."

"Yes, I am and thank you so much for meeting us today."

She gave me a hug and said, "I'm so glad you finally got your mother in here."

Dr. Webster immediately went over to Mom and introduced herself and invited us into her office.

In the office, she gave Mom a hug and held her hands. "Irene, Nancy told me about your HIV infection from the blood transfusion you received. I'm so sorry," she said warmly.

"Aren't you afraid of me?" Mom asked in a shaky voice. "You're holding my hands. What if I'm contagious?"

"Irene, you are not contagious. I work with HIV patients all day and I don't worry about catching AIDS from them," she responded.

Dad and I left Mom and Dr. Webster alone for about fifteen minutes. Mom came out with a smile on her face. I was so delighted. I hadn't seen a smile on Mom's face since she was diagnosed. How she needed the warmth and support Dr. Webster could give her.

Mom walked over to us. "I'm making an appointment to see Ann next week," she told us.

I thought they must have had quite a conversation and developed a relationship quickly as Mom was calling Dr. Webster by her first name.

Mom left the hospital a new woman. She had found a friend…someone with whom she could share. She had many friends at home. However, Mom always made up excuses why she was unable to see them. Her friends from the Garden Club frequently called to visit. She didn't know what to say to them and was afraid they would discover she was infected with HIV if they visited. She also didn't want to lie to them. So she kept her illness a secret. People were confused by her uncharacteristic behavior.

Even her closest friends were being pushed away. How she needed them for support and caring but the risk of telling them or visiting with them was too threatening to her. She would rather suffer in silence than reveal her frightening secret.

Dr. Webster agreed to see Mom in an individual session instead of in a support group with other women. Each week Dad would take her to visit Dr. Webster. Mom felt such a feeling of love and acceptance from her sessions with her.

I remember Mom coming back from an appointment at the Mind/Body Clinic and saying that Ann had encouraged her to pursue her passion for painting. The following week Mom signed up for a painting course in our town. She was so excited to be participating in something that brought her joy. However, after three lessons, Mom decided she would have to discontinue her lessons because she suffered from ataxia that affected her balance. It caused her to feel unsteady on her feet. She felt embarrassed and discontinued her lessons.

At the Mind/Body Clinic, Dr. Webster helped her cope with her negative feelings. Mom constantly worried about what people would think of her if they only knew she was HIV-positive. She looked forward to her visits with Ann. Her negative attitude always changed after a visit with her. How grateful I felt that we had found this wonderful woman who listened to her fears and concerns with heartfelt understanding. She was someone Mom could confide in and share her deepest fears. Before Thanksgiving, Mom was worried about being with her niece who was pregnant at the time. She was concerned that she might be contagious to her. Dr. Webster assured Mom that her HIV infection would not be harmful to a pregnant woman.

At the clinic, she was given a guided imagery meditation tape to listen to daily. Mom wasn't used to meditating. However, she knew that I meditated and had used various relaxation techniques to cope with my medical conditions. At first, she didn't want to listen to anything that I suggested, but one day after my yoga class, I stopped by her house. She was obviously depressed. I had to figure out a way to humor her. I decided to show her one of the yoga exercises we had done in class that day. It was called the lion pose. She started laughing hysterically when she saw my mouth open and my tongue stick out as far as it could. My eyes were wide open like I was in a state of surprise. It was quite a sight. That was the first time I had seen her really laugh since her diagnosis. "Mom, this pose will reduce any tension in your facial muscles and jaw," I explained. I had to find ways to amuse her and yet help ease the stress that was controlling her mind and body.

That day I also taught her abdominal breathing. She was used to breathing from her chest instead of her abdomen. Mom's shallow breathing exacerbated her anxiety. She started taking deep breaths by inhaling through her nose and imagining her stomach was extending out, then on the exhalation she would exhale through her mouth and pull her abdomen back in. I had her do several of these deep breathing exercises and she continued to do them periodically through the day. It brought her relief from some of the anxiety she was experiencing.

Mom was so anxious that it was difficult for her to really focus on any tape at this time. Since I knew many other methods of relaxation, I felt that she would benefit from progressive tensing of each muscle group. First, I instructed her to tense her left hand and arm for a few seconds and then release. Then I told her to tense the muscles in her right arm and hand for several seconds and then let go. She followed my instructions and continued tensing each part of her body and then relaxing. She seemed to find this type of technique helpful.

"This will help you fall asleep faster. Each time you tense a muscle and release, the muscles become more relaxed," I told her.

Since I had made visualization tapes for myself and other people, I decided to make one for Mom. It was imperative to keep her T-cell count elevated to ward off any opportunistic infections. I recorded a visualization tape where she would first begin with a few deep breaths and then imagine herself by the ocean that she enjoyed so much and feel the sun shining down on her. Next, I told her to picture her thymus gland producing hundreds of T-cells that would travel throughout her body fighting off any opportunistic infections. I then instructed her to visualize healing white light pouring down from above into her head and into every cell in her body. Doing this allowed her to take a pro-active approach to her dreadful illness. She had to take charge and not let the HIV infection control her.

Mom enjoyed listening to the personalized visualization tape I made for her. When I visited her one evening, I saw Mom sitting in the rocking chair with earphones to her walkman on her head.

Dad said, "Nancy, I don't know what you did to Mom. But she won't take those earphones off. She listens to that visualization tape several times a day. I never thought she would agree to doing something like that. But it sure is helping her."

I was so thankful that the holistic mind/body techniques I was teaching Mom had a positive effect on her physical and emotional health. At least she felt some control over her illness. I also felt that she would benefit from some music therapy. She enjoyed my piano playing. I recorded a piano tape of me playing her favorites including some of the old standards by Cole Porter, George Gershwin, and Richard Rodgers and Oscar Hammerstein. Every night before she went to bed, Dad had to put the piano tape in the recorder to help her fall asleep. The music had a healing effect on her immune system as well as lifting her spirits and bringing her into a more positive state of mind. This induced a sense of well-being and relaxation. I knew a positive connection between her body and mind could be salubrious for her condition.

She would also listen to the imagery tape that Dr. Webster had given her. Each day she was faithful to doing these mind/body techniques.

After a week, Dad called me and said, "Nancy, you were successful in convincing Mom about the holistic relaxation techniques. She certainly seems to be enjoying it. I never thought she would become a believer in this type of healing. I have to admit you certainly changed her view on meditation and visualization. She seems more in control of her emotions when listening to the tapes," he said.

I was sitting with her one night when she reminisced about her trip out West. She and Dad had enjoyed a six week trip to visit the National Parks, which included the Grand Canyon, Yellowstone Park, Bryce Canyon, and several others. My father had asked me to help make reservations. I was able to get good airline fares for them. They left six months after Mom's heart surgery. But Mom still wasn't feeling well at the time. That didn't stop them. They were gone for six weeks, traveling all around California, Arizona, Nevada, and Utah.

Floyd and I had picked Mom and Dad up at the airport on their arrival home. Mom and Dad met us in the baggage area. How tired she looked when I first saw her. She walked over to me and said, "Nancy, I feel so sick. All I want to do is go home and sleep in my own bed. I felt awful during our trip."

The virus must have started to affect her shortly after her blood transfusion because she complained of fevers and fatigue within three weeks after her surgery. This didn't prevent them from going on the long-awaited vacation. Since Dad had looked forward to this trip so much, both he and Mom decided to go anyway hoping that Mom would feel better traveling and seeing new sights. After their return, her health continued to decline. Even though she communicated these symptoms to her doctors, it didn't seem to matter. No doctor suspected HIV infection in a sixty-six-year old woman. She went undiagnosed for five years.

* * *

After Mom was diagnosed with HIV infection in 1988, she continued to try to lead a fairly normal life even though she often felt ill with swollen glands and a low grade fever. Mom continued to battle her illness for the next two and a half years. For the following two winters, Mom and Dad traveled to their Florida home where they could enjoy their mobile home and bask in the Florida sunshine.

One Christmas, before she left for Florida, she was able to host her annual Christmas Eve party. This was a tradition that Mom cherished. She spent days preparing all of the food herself. Her festive dining room table was covered with casserole dishes that included chicken pie, beef pie, ham, scalloped potatoes, vegetables and an assortment of different desserts including everyone's favorite lemon meringue pie, apricot pie and her delicious strawberry angel cake with whipped cream. Two weeks after Christmas Mom and Dad left for Florida.

Three months later in March, I flew down to visit with them for a week. While I was there, the community had planned a St. Patrick's Day party at the clubhouse. Mom hadn't slept more than a few hours a night when I was visiting. Her eyes were red and tired. At the party, Dad and Mom introduced me to their friends. I was amazed how Mom could conceal her illness with a smile. I knew she was putting on a good facade so no one would suspect she was ill. She was so fatigued, but Dad wanted to partake in the festivities of the St. Patrick's Day party. Mom didn't want to disappoint him and she wanted to make my visit enjoyable. Pretending I was having a good time drained me emotionally.

Mom and I did get to spend several days sitting in the yard reading, relaxing and just talking. Some days Mom felt better than others. One day we even enjoyed a few hours at the beach. Mom didn't go swimming but she sat in her beach chair with her white sun hat and beach jacket and read a book while Dad and I dodged the waves in the rough Atlantic surf. Mom took a picture of Dad and me having fun in the waves. They had taught me to swim at the age of six. I remember my father throwing me in the waves with my life jacket on when I was a young child. From then on, I felt like a fish in the ocean.

A month later, they decided to come back home. Mom's 50th year high school reunion was coming up in the summer and she hesitated about attending this event that always brought her so much joy and laughter. She had been a member of the reunion committee for many years. However, this year was different. Mom didn't know whether she would feel well enough to attend this very important milestone. Dr. Webster encouraged her to buy a dress in case she did make the decision to attend. She had never missed a reunion and it meant so much to her. That day, she called me up to tell me she was going to attend the reunion. Mom said, "Nancy, I'm worried about using a cane at the reunion, but I might need one for balance."

"Don't worry about that. Many people your age use canes for support for a bad knee, hip, back or some other medical condition."

Mom also worried about walking at the reunion because of her unsteady balance. She didn't want people to think she had been drinking.

She called me the following day and said that she had a wonderful time at the gathering and socializing with her friends she cared for so much. She was happy she had attended and had enjoyed being with her former classmates.

During that same summer, Mom's health began to decline rapidly. It was 1990 and Floyd, Tom, Shawn, and I had made plans to travel to Canterbury, England to visit my pen pal, Sharon, whom I had been corresponding with for a couple of years. Floyd and I were planning on celebrating our 20th wedding anniversary in England.

Realizing we would be gone for almost two weeks concerned me. Mom had been having some dreadful days and was plagued with frequent fevers and a lingering cough. She didn't have much strength and spent most of her time in bed. We decided to go anyway, hoping that she would be all right until we returned home. We were trying to lead a normal life even though we were worried about Mom's condition.

Dad brought us to the airport and we arrived in London the next morning. None of us had slept on the plane. After taking the bus to the car rental office, we left London for Canterbury. About thirty minutes into our ride to Sharon's house, I said to Floyd, "Where did you put Shawn's crutches?"

"I thought you had them."

"Well, they're not in the back seat," I replied. After checking the trunk packed with suitcases and Shawn's wheelchair, we realized we had left them at the car rental office. On the way back, we all laughed at Floyd trying to navigate driving on the left hand side of the road and attempting to maneuver the rotary by the car rental office. When we arrived back at the rental office, we noticed the crutches were exactly where we had left them.

We made our way to Sharon's house near the Canterbury Cathedral. Sharon, her husband, and two daughters were so delighted to meet us. They gave us a tour of Canterbury that afternoon.

I was still worried about Mom and wondered if she was all right.

Even though Sharon lived in another country, I couldn't seem to share with her about my mother's HIV infection. She talked about people with AIDS. Yet, I still remained silent. I planned to call Mom and Dad a couple of times during our trip to make sure nothing had happened to her.

We stayed with Sharon for a few days while they escorted us around Canterbury. On July 4th, we took the train into London. We had planned to do some sightseeing. Tom pushed Shawn in his wheelchair as we toured the inside of St. Paul's Cathedral where Prince Charles and Princess Diana were married. We visited Westminster Abbey where kings and queens are crowned. By the time we arrived at Buckingham Palace, we were exhausted from so much walking. We decided to rest in Trafalgar Square. We listened to Big Ben ring on the hour. After visiting many historical sights in London, we headed to the train station for our trip back to Canterbury. Later that day, I called Dad to see how Mom was feeling. Dad answered the phone. He was delighted to hear from us.

Anxiously, I asked, "How has Mom been feeling? Is she still having head pain?"

"Nancy, her condition hasn't changed much since you left for vacation. She's sleeping right now."

I felt relieved, knowing that her health hadn't deteriorated in the past week. After touring England and Wales during the next few days, we drove back to Sharon's house. We wanted to spend our last few days visiting them. I sat in the living room with Sharon wondering whether to share with her that my mother was infected with HIV. After all, we had been corresponding for two years and I hadn't said anything. I hadn't confided in anyone at this time except our family. I decided not to share what we had been going through.

We left for Boston the next day. Dad was going to pick us up at the airport. We all had a wonderful time on our vacation, but I was looking forward to flying back home to spend time with Mom.

~ 4 ~

Stormy Days

We arrived home from London late Sunday morning. Monday afternoon I drove down to visit Mom and Dad. She was sitting in her lounge chair in the family room. I kissed Mom on her forehead. She was so glad to see me again and asked questions about our trip to England. When I first walked into the family room, I noticed Mom looking through the newspaper as if she were searching for something. "Were you looking for something in the newspaper, Mom?"

"I'm trying to find any news on HIV and AIDS. I can't find anything today," she uttered sadly. She looked so tired. The volume on the television was blaring. She had a moderate loss of hearing and usually had the volume turned up on the television. It was four o'clock and she was eating some custard pudding Dad had made for her. I walked into the kitchen to make myself a cup of tea.

As Dad was cleaning up the kitchen area, I asked, "Does she always scrutinize the newspaper like that?"

"Yes, Nancy, she does. That's her routine. Every afternoon she keeps asking me if the newspaper has arrived. She examines each page to see if there are any new breakthroughs, treatments, or cures for HIV and AIDS," Dad replied. "After she reads through the paper, she's tired and usually goes to bed to rest. She listens to your music tape or the visualization one you made for her. That seems to bring her so much relief."

I went back into the family room. Mom's eyes were closed and her head was leaning to one side. She had been attempting to stay awake until the newspaper came. I sat on the couch and sipped my tea while I watched Mom sitting in the chair. Suddenly, she opened her eyes and looked at me. She asked me all kinds of questions about our trip to England and Wales. I told her some of the sights we saw. Then she said, "Nancy, I forgot to tell you that the other night when I was watching the news on television, I saw Princess Diana with some AIDS patients. She was holding a baby with AIDS. She was shaking hands with other AIDS patients at a hospital that she was visiting."

"Yes, I know that Princess Diana is an advocate for AIDS. I read that she opened up the first AIDS hospital ward in the United Kingdom."

Here was a princess, charming and respected, and reaching out to those stigmatized due to AIDS. People with HIV or AIDS were often discriminated against and considered "dirty." A royal, elegant woman, holding a baby with AIDS in her arms showed love and compassion…not fear or disgrace. Showing her concern for their welfare and giving them the affection AIDS victims so desperately needed sent a message to the world that there was no reason for any stigma or discrimination. Mom was touched by the sight of seeing Princess Diana shaking hands with AIDS victims and not being afraid to touch them.

"See, Mom, she isn't afraid to touch people who have HIV or AIDS. So you shouldn't feel contaminated. She's not wearing gloves or concerned about reaching out to them and touching them," I said.

Mom stared at the floor. "I know that, Nancy, but I'm still afraid of what our friends would think of me."

"It was just a horrible medical tragedy, Mom."

"But look what they did to those Florida boys who had hemophilia. They were HIV-positive and people burned their house," she said, referring to the Ray family whose sons had hemophilia and were infected with HIV from contaminated blood-clotting factor.

"Unfortunately, there are some people who don't understand this illness and are frightened by it," I said. "Many people need to be educated about HIV and AIDS. I'm sure there are many people who would support you. Look how Mother Teresa has helped AIDS victims and has even set up clinics for them." Shawn and I were fortunate enough to see Mother Teresa when she came to Boston. I pushed Shawn's wheelchair through the crowd to see her walk by us. People like Mother Teresa and Princess Diana were reaching out to society to try to show compassion to people who were fighting this ghastly disease that was taking the lives of people throughout the world.

Mom's obsessive search for AIDS information had led me to research the disease on my own. In July 1981, the New York Times had reported an outbreak of a rare form of cancer among homosexual men in New York City and San Francisco. Kaposi's sarcoma was so rare that few doctors had ever seen it. Now, as outbreaks became common, it was referred to as "gay cancer". However, it was medically known as Kaposi's sarcoma.

During that time, New York City emergency rooms were seeing outwardly appearing healthy young men with flu-like symptoms, fevers, swollen lymph nodes, and a rare type of pneumonia called *Pneumocystis.*

Later, in 1982, this mysterious disease was now being called GRID by the Centers for Disease Control. GRID stood for Gay-Related Immune Deficiency. But soon doctors in New York City were seeing sick babies and hemophiliacs. A baby had died in late 1982 from numerous blood transfusions that were contaminated with the virus. As it became obvious that the syndrome was not limited to homosexual men, scientists at the CDC created the name AIDS which stood for "acquired immune deficiency syndrome."

While I was watching the news one day in 1985, health officials were announcing a test to detect HIV infection in the blood supply. I listened to the startling number of people affected with AIDS. By March 1985, the epidemic was raging in our nation and other parts of the world. The newscaster stated that thousands of Americans had already died of AIDS or were infected with HIV. Sadly, few people seemed to pay much attention to the disease because it really wasn't affecting people they knew.

In 1987, I called the American Red Cross and was concerned about my own safety since I had received a transfusion during a six-hour hysterectomy in February of 1985. They assured me saying, "Don't worry because we would have notified you if you had been infected." I hung up the telephone feeling relieved that everything was all right. I had no symptoms, but I was concerned. My doctor told me there was no need to be tested since my blood count was normal and he saw no need for further testing. Fortunately, I was not infected with the virus. But many people were becoming infected and the Red Cross was not notifying the recipients that they could have been exposed to HIV contaminated blood through a transfusion.

It had been six years since this new virus had come to the attention of the medical community. Each year more and more people were becoming infected. These people included homosexuals, hemophiliacs, transfused patients, drug abusers, and babies born to HIV-positive women. There was definite evidence that AIDS was a blood-borne disease. The question remains, "Why didn't our government develop a serious prevention strategy knowing that large numbers of Americans were becoming infected with a virus that would eventually weaken their immune system and make them open to opportunistic diseases that would eventually kill them?"

Why did some reporters *sleep* when our country was five years into a disease that had already taken thousands of lives? Many news reporters seemed afraid to mention the word AIDS on television because it was usually equated with the homosexual community. Did people really want to hear about a disease that was affecting gays? After all, gays were stigmatized. Many people thought no one would want to hear more stories about their mysterious virus that was causing so many people to become seriously ill. It was almost if they didn't want to hear anything about this bizarre illness that was killing people.

President Ronald Reagan was very reticent to discuss the subject of AIDS, even though many government scientists pleaded with the administration to provide funds for research. The sad part is that these scientists were ignored because some people felt little would be gained from researching a "gay disease." President Reagan made his first speech on AIDS in 1987 after approximately 21,000 Americans had died of this killer virus. So many people died needlessly due to the administration's lack of concern about AIDS.

I felt angry and saddened that our country did not take aggressive measures early on in fighting this disease that was plaguing our nation. I felt betrayed by the blood banks and the Red Cross as they failed to inform my mother that one of the donors who she received blood from had AIDS. By failing to notify Mom of the possibility that she could have been infected with HIV, Dad had been put at risk of becoming infected himself. Dad said he called the Red Cross after Mom's diagnosis to find the name of the donor. However, because of confidentiality, they could not release his name except to confirm that he had been infected with the virus and came from New York. Thankfully, Dad was tested three times and was not infected with HIV.

Dad and I stared at Mom as she rested in her lounge chair. She was depressed that the daily newspaper hadn't reported any new breakthroughs in AIDS research. Dad went over to place a blanket on Mom. But again, she opened her eyes and began talking to us.

"Nancy, how are Shawn and Tom?"

"Shawn's excited about his drum lessons. He just bought a new drum set last week and practices about an hour a day. Tom finished his cross country meets and came in second in the last competition of the year."

"What good news," Mom said excitedly. "I remember watching Tom race in several cross country meets. I was so proud of him," she said with a gleam in her eye. "Oh, that's wonderful. Please congratulate them for me," Mom replied.

"Yes, Mom, I'll tell them tonight when we go out for pizza."

* * *

Memories began to flood my mind of the wonderful times Mom had with her grandchildren. When my parents were living at Cape Cod during the summer, we would often go down to visit them. One summer, when Shawn was a newborn, we rented a cottage in the same town where they were staying. The bitter, cold New England winter was over. A flamboyant spring had made its exit leaving us the summer months to enjoy. I had waited in eager anticipation for this special family vacation for several months. The gentle lapping of the ocean waves against the shore, the sea gulls chirping songs of delight, the amber sunset resting over Cape Cod Bay…the perfect setting to relax after a seemingly long pregnancy. Tom was three and Shawn was two months old.

One sunny, hot and windy afternoon, Mom and Dad came over to our cottage to spend the afternoon with us. She bought Tom a kite to fly. As soon as we arrived at the beach, Tom ran up to Mom and started pulling his grandmother's hand.

"Let's go fly the kite now," he said excitedly.

"Okay Tom, let's see if we can get this kite to take off." They both ran off together. After a few unsuccessful attempts, Mom finally got the red kite off the ground and soaring in the air. They both enjoyed flying the kite along the long stretch of sandy beach.

"Wow, look how high my kite is flying," Tom shouted with glee. Dad, Floyd and I sat in our beach chairs watching them have fun. Mom enjoyed helping Tom make elaborate sand castles.

Later, in the afternoon, Dad and Mom chuckled as they watched Tom trying desperately to amuse his new baby brother. Unsuccessful in his attempts, Tom turned his attention to me. I had been resting in my comfortable chair and really didn't want to be disturbed.

"Mom...let's go swimming," he shouted, boisterously. Filled with robust energy despite several hours in the sun, he tugged relentlessly at my arm. As I attempted to get out of my beach chair, I found myself too weak to pull myself up. Floyd noticed my difficulty and quickly offered his help. My body wracked with pain.

"Maybe I'm still weak from giving birth to Shawn," I say to Floyd.

"But Nancy, it's been almost three months. You should be feeling stronger, not weaker. I really think you should be seen by another doctor. Maybe this time something will show up."

Nights brought sleepless, agonizing hours. The sheets on my toes and feet brought excruciating pain. The bedroom reeked of Bengay. Nothing brought relief. We decided to go home early so I could be seen by another physician. This would be the seventh doctor I had seen in the past four months.

I was examined by an internist. He took a blood sample and a week later called me with the results. I tested positive for rheumatoid arthritis. Tired of feeling weak and sore all the time, I told Dr. Robbins that I would like to be seen by a rheumatologist. The following day I received a phone call from a Dr. Ackerman. After relaying my symptoms to him over the telephone, he said, "I think I have a good idea what's causing your problem. I'd like to see you tomorrow at noon."

The next day, after a comprehensive two hour examination and several blood tests, Dr. Ackerman said in a concerned voice, "Mrs. Draper, the blood tests indicated what's causing your muscular weakness and pain. But I'd like to explain your condition to both you and your husband together."

Together? Was it that serious? I worried. Floyd walked into the examining room and sat down beside me as Dr. Ackerman began to explain.

"Along with the rheumatoid arthritis, that is affecting your joints you have a muscle disease called polymyositis. It's very unusual to see this illness in a twenty-nine year old woman."

"Polymyosititis…is that like polio?" I asked.

"No, it isn't anything like polio, but it's a very serious muscle disease. What you really have is a 'fire' in your body because of so much inflammation. We have to suppress the illness before it permanently damages your muscles. Hopefully, steroids will reduce the inflammation in your body and bring your muscle enzyme level down."

Could this really be happening? I had just delivered a baby four months ago, and now I had two young boys to take care of. How could I be a good mother when I couldn't even tie Tommy's shoes due to the rheumatoid arthritis? The polymyositis made it difficult to climb stairs and do simple everyday tasks. However, after being on the prednisone for a few months, I began to feel much better. The blood levels were lower and I was going into remission.

Soon our fears shifted to Shawn. One Sunday night, Mom and Dad came over to the house for dinner. Mom noticed Shawn lying limply on the floor. "Nancy, has Shawn started to crawl yet?" she asked.

"No, Mom. But I have mentioned our concerns to Shawn's pediatrician. He doesn't think there's any problem. He told us that Shawn is developmentally delayed because of the early delivery." Floyd and I constantly wondered why he wasn't making the milestones that Tom or other babies his age could do. The reassurance from our pediatrician failed to alleviate our fears. Something was wrong and we had to find out what it was. Mom suggested that we seek further medical testing for Shawn. I made an appointment with a doctor in Boston.

Two weeks later, on the morning of the appointment I awoke to beams of sunlight shimmering beneath the window shade awakening me from a very light sleep. Surprised that I had managed to doze off for a couple of hours, my thoughts immediately began to dwell on the ominous news we would probably receive today. I stared at Floyd lying beside me. Today was his 30th birthday! But I feared we would not be in a festive mood. This morning we were taking Shawn to Boston to see a specialist that had been recommended to us. Shawn was fifteen months old and still unable to sit up alone.

When we arrived at the doctor's office, Shawn sat peacefully on Floyd's lap while I answered questions involving my pregnancy and delivery. She briefly examined him and then gave the diagnosis. "I'm afraid that Shawn has spastic quadriplegic cerebral palsy. Mrs. Draper, from what you told me concerning Shawn's birth, it seems your placenta was only fifty percent effective. This prevented Shawn from receiving enough food and oxygen which caused some areas of his brain to be affected. These areas control his motor ability. It certainly doesn't seem like Shawn's intelligence or speech has been affected. He is very alert and bright."

I wasn't surprised at Dr. Cook's diagnosis. I had suspected Shawn had some form of cerebral palsy from my own research. "I want you to understand that Shawn does not have an illness but he has a condition that anyone could get through a head trauma at any age."

Floyd and I looked at each other. We both knew the worst thing we could do was to sit home and feel self-pity. We wouldn't want him to feel that way when he was older. Instead, we decided to take action and began searching for some type of help for Shawn. I had learned from coping with my medical conditions that no one comes to hold your hand to help. One has to research and learn how to be resourceful. We worked with the hospital social worker and made many phone calls on our own. After two weeks we finally found a program that would send a physical therapist and teacher to our house.

How did all this happen to us? Only seven years ago, Floyd and I were happily walking down the church aisle, glowing at the thought of sharing our life together. Now we wondered what preparation we possessed to cope with these difficulties. At first, I asked, "Why me?" But after considerable thought, I concluded, "Why not me?" Was I better than the next person? Should I be exempt from the trials of life? Everyone is certain to experience hardships in life and our family was no exception. Life is not always going to be sunny; there will be days when it will be stormy. Somehow, we would have to endure these stormy days. Instead of believing the load was unfair, it was necessary to find a way to face these hardships.

Feeling sorry for ourselves wasn't going to make it any easier. No one likes to suffer. While we do not choose to suffer we can choose how we will react to that suffering. Floyd and I chose to face our difficulties with faith that together we could face our problems with God's help.

We stopped at my parents' house on the way home. They had been taking care of Tom while we were at the doctor's office. Mom and Dad were upset about the diagnosis, but relieved that we finally knew what was causing Shawn's delay in sitting and walking.

Mom always enjoyed playing with Shawn and reading books to him. My father said he wanted to make a desk for Shawn to make it easier for him to do paper work and play educational games with the teacher. Shawn was starting his education at the age of sixteen months. Little did we know that his early education intervention would pay off later in life. Shawn is now a practicing attorney.

51

Mom had always told me to be persistent and never give up. She taught me how to have faith in myself. Now, several years later, Mom was diagnosed with HIV. She was a fighter but had been through so much. She didn't know if she had the energy to fight this painful and frightening illness. Floyd and I had plenty of experience in dealing with medical adversity. We knew somehow we could help Mom deal with this terrible tragedy.

~ 5 ~

Neurological Damage

Since her devastating diagnosis, Mom had been suffering from loneliness and severe depression. Mom and Dad had been discussing traveling to Florida for the winter. Dad thought the sunshine and warmer temperatures would boost Mom's mental state. They had always enjoyed being with their friends and spending time at the ocean. This trip would be different. Unfortunately, Mom was too weak to swim and traveling to Florida by car would be too physically draining for her.

"Dad, I have an idea. You can drive down to Florida and Mom and I can fly down a few days after you leave," I suggested. "That would give you time to get the house ready for her."

"Who would take care of Mom while I was gone?" he asked. He was concerned because Mom's balance had deteriorated. "She will need someone to be with her. I'm afraid she might fall."

"Dad, that's not a problem. I could cancel my piano lessons and stay with Mom. Then we could fly down after you have settled into the house."

"That's a wonderful idea. Are you sure it will be okay with Floyd?" he asked.

"Yes, Dad, I have already discussed it with him, and he agreed it was a perfect idea. I'll call the airlines tonight to schedule a flight for us."

After dinner that evening, I called several airlines searching for a bargain airfare for us during the third week in January. After several calls, I made reservations with Delta to fly into West Palm Beach.

As soon as the reservation was made, I phoned Dad to confirm that everything was all arranged and gave him the schedule and details of the flight. He was so relieved and looking forward to relaxing in the sun with Mom.

"By the way, Nancy, I forgot to mention to you that Mom has an appointment with the neurologist tomorrow afternoon at two o'clock. Would it be possible for you to come with us?"

I attended as many appointments as I could with Mom and Dad, and they appreciated me being their advocate. "I'm sorry Dad, but actually I have a doctor's exam myself tomorrow afternoon. I'm afraid I won't be able to accompany you this time."

"Oh, don't worry about not coming," he responded. "We shouldn't have any problems."

The next day, as I was putting away the dinner dishes, the telephone rang. It was Dad. He was extremely angry.

"What's the matter?" I asked, worried that Mom had become sicker.

"Nancy, you can't believe how Dr. Johnson upset Mom today during her visit! You know how concerned Mom is about someone catching HIV from her. She told Dr. Johnson she is worried that if someone visits her they might become infected. But Dr. Johnson emphatically stated that the only way she could infect another person would be through blood contact or sexual relations. He assured her that a person could not contract HIV or AIDS from a hug, kiss, drinking from the same glass or casual contact. After he comforted her with this explanation, she seemed relieved."

"I don't understand...then why was she so disturbed?"

"When he took her blood pressure, he put on latex gloves before he touched her. No other doctor has ever used gloves for such a simple procedure. She was confused and distraught."

"Did Mom say anything to him?"

"Even though Mom was frightened, she spoke up to Dr. Johnson. She asked him why he was using gloves to take her blood pressure after he had just told her she wasn't contagious," Dad said.

"What did he say to her?"

"Well, he didn't answer. He just walked over to his nurse who was standing near the doorway and I overheard him ask her to finish the tests. She didn't wear gloves. There was no blood involved, so there was no danger."

His thoughtlessness increased Mom's anxiety about her HIV infection. She began to feel *dirtier* because of the treatment she received from him.

Dad attempted to calm Mom after the appointment, but Mom's confidence was shattered after her visit. The explanation of her not being contagious was negated by his obvious fear of contagion and his insolent manner. This was the only appointment I had been unable to attend with my parents. They needed an advocate since many of the doctors were not treating Mom with the respect she deserved.

"Mom has one more doctor's visit next Friday. Can you come with us?" he asked. This would be her last medical appointment before we left for Florida.

"Yes, Dad, I don't have any piano lessons or other appointments that day, so I'll be able to go with you and Mom." I hadn't scheduled anything because I knew this would be an important doctor's visit.

Mom was going to be seeing her internist who was a specialist in HIV/AIDS. My father had been trying to persuade Mom to agree to hire a housekeeper to stay with her for a few hours a day as a respite for him. This would also give him time to do errands such as food shopping. Mom feared that if someone came in the house, the person would have to be informed of her infection. Dad discussed the matter with Dr. Miller before she examined Mom in hopes she could convince Mom to agree to such an arrangement.

After Dr. Miller examined Mom, she wheeled her into her office where Dad and I were waiting. My mother sat in her wheelchair as Dr. Miller chided Mom for not allowing a housekeeper to help out at home.

"Irene, the cytomegalovirus has attacked your brain. You know this is one of the opportunistic infections that indicate AIDS. The CMV will affect your ability to do any housework. You can't expect your husband to do it all!" Feeling berated, Mom lowered her head like a little child who had been scolded for misbehaving. She hung her head and began sobbing.

Poor Mom…being told by Dr. Miller that the CMV had invaded her brain affected her dramatically. She dreaded the possibility that HIV would cause neurological damage such as dementia and ataxia. She was frightened that the CMV would eventually deteriorate her cognitive abilities. She left the office feeling even worse than when she had come in.

When we left, Mom was still weeping. It was a windy, rainy winter day in Boston. Dad looked at us and said, "Why don't you both wait here and I'll get the car. Meet me at the entrance." He left us in the hospital lobby while I tried to console Mom. She was such an intelligent woman and was facing losing her ability to talk, think, and walk.

People were passing by, wondering what was happening. Mom had become so despondent and kept asking questions.

"Nancy, you heard Dr. Miller say I was going to lose my mind," she cried as she sat waiting for my father to come back. "What am I going to do?"

I kept searching for tissues in my pocketbook to wipe her tears. She sat hopelessly in her wheelchair. The expression on her face revealed she knew the battle was almost over. She had just been told that she now had CMV and that it was one of the opportunistic infections that indicate the diagnosis of full-blown AIDS. She was devastated.

She stumbled over words as she attempted to express her emotions to me. The possibility of losing her mental facilities was desperately terrifying to her. She was afraid of deteriorating into helplessness.

I attempted to soften the blow. I felt it was unnecessary to be so blunt with Mom in her fragile physical and emotional state. Dr. Miller cared deeply for Mom and was trying to help, but lacked tactfulness. Maybe she thought it was the only way to get through to her.

Bitter that Mom had to endure such negativity from another doctor, I tried to explain to her that the cytomegalovirus hadn't affected her brain significantly and would not cause any immediate changes. But my reassurances were futile. All she felt was panic and depression. She didn't say much during the hour drive home. I sat in the back seat feeling completely devoid of any energy. We stopped at a seafood restaurant to eat. She stared at me throughout the meal.

I started experiencing sharp chest pains during dinner. I did some deep breathing and eventually, the pain subsided, but my chest muscles felt tense and sore. Mom was worried about me as she knew I wasn't feeling well. In fact, she always worried about her only daughter. I tried to pretend I was okay…but when I couldn't eat my dinner, she was concerned about my health.

The stress of keeping Mom's HIV status a secret and not being allowed to share with my friends that Mom was dying of AIDS was hurtful and distressing. The secrecy had been causing a strain on our marriage since Floyd was the only person I could really share my fears and concerns with. I knew how much he loved Mom. However, he didn't want to discuss it as much as I needed. I had no one else to go to for support. It was too depressing for him to dwell on it day after day. I understood his feelings. It wasn't fair to him to bear the brunt of my depression and anxiety. He had his own work to deal with. Even though he was very supportive, I needed other friends to share this burden with.

After lunch, Dad talked about going to Florida in the next three weeks and seemed excited about it. I had my summer clothes and some heavy sweaters packed since it would still be fairly cool in the evenings. The following weeks went by quickly.

Floyd took me to stay with Mom the day Dad was ready to leave. Mom was sitting in her favorite lounge chair as she watched Dad get his bags packed. He explained everything I needed to know about her medications and schedule. Before he left, Dad came in the family room to kiss Mom good-bye. She seemed very satisfied with the arrangement of my staying with her and flying down to Florida in a few days.

"Drive safely," she instructed him as he walked toward the front door with his suitcases. Immediately after Dad left, Mom went to her bedroom to take a nap. I had brought some books and relaxation tapes for my own benefit as well as hers. I decided I would rest on the couch near her bedroom as I knew it would be a difficult four days taking care of her.

When she awoke from her nap, she asked, "Where's Dad? Did he go food shopping tonight?"

"Mom, don't you remember that he left for Florida this afternoon? You know he's driving to your home in Florida and we'll be going down in a few days."

"Where is Florida?"

My heart sank. I couldn't believe her mental state had deteriorated so quickly. It was heartbreaking to see her so confused.

Dad called around eight o'clock that evening and wanted to talk to Mom. Just a few hours after Dad had left Mom had become disoriented.

I was hesitant to put her on the phone for fear it would frighten my father. Earlier in the day, she appeared jovial and kidded with him. I couldn't believe the drastic change in her mental state in just a few hours. She spoke to Dad for a couple of minutes but couldn't make sense of what he was saying. After they finished the conversation, she asked, "Why is he going to Florida?"

However, later that evening she was lucid and carried on an intelligent conversation. She even answered questions on a game show. When it was over, she was tired and I helped her to bed.

Dad had set up an intercom system between his bedroom and Mom's. He wanted to be able to listen if he heard her calling during the night. She needed help walking to the bathroom. She suffered from vertigo and required physical support so she wouldn't lose her balance and fall. He had also given her a little bell to ring to alert him if she needed help.

"Listen, Mom, if you need me for anything during the night I want you to use the intercom or ring the bell and I'll come to your room. I don't want you to get up by yourself to use the bathroom unless you call me. Do you understand?"

"I promise," she responded obediently.

"Good girl, Mom," I said as I kissed her on the forehead before I left her bedroom. I had noticed the Bible on her bureau next to the bed. She had been reading from it to gain some strength and peace.

That evening I had the intercom on in my father's bedroom and heard a loud noise from Mom's bedroom. I immediately dashed into her room to see what had happened. She was sprawled out on the floor by her bed. Looking at the clock, I saw it was 3:00 a.m. I attempted to pick her up and put her back into bed, but I wasn't strong enough. My efforts kept failing and I didn't know if I would have to call Floyd to assist me. I knew I had to devise a strategy to get her back into her bed.

"Mom, why didn't you call me?" I asked.

She replied, "I'm sorry, Nancy, but I had to get to the bathroom and I didn't want to bother you." I noticed that the floor was a little damp.

Trying not to sound upset with her, I said, "But Mom, that's why I told you to ring the bell or call me on the intercom." I continued to lift her but being only five feet tall and weighing less than 110 pounds didn't give me much leverage. Finally, after fifteen minutes and several unsuccessful attempts, I managed to push her up against the bed and roll her back on her bed. I changed her nightie and covered her with blankets.

Weak from the stress and the physical strain of lifting Mom, I found myself unable to walk back to my bedroom. The only way I could manage to reach my bedroom was to crawl on my hands and knees. My muscles were so weak and caused difficulty walking. I feared the polymyositis might be flaring up again. I was experiencing the same symptoms of weak, sore muscles throughout my body. I knew I would have to have a muscle enzyme blood test to determine if I was in a flare-up and needed to go on prednisone again.

Not now...there was too much to do for Mom. There is no one else to take care of her in such an intimate way, I thought to myself.

I crawled back into bed, but was unable to sleep. I had to keep vigilant. *What if this happens again?* I didn't know if I would be able to get her back into her bed. Besides, she could get hurt or even bleed from an injury. Blood was something I had to be constantly aware of for fear of infecting myself. If any blood were involved, I would certainly have to use gloves. The intercom was beside my bed and I was listening intently in case I heard any noise from her room. I fought the sleep my body so desperately needed. However, early in the morning, my body lost the battle to stay awake, and I managed to get at least two hours of sleep before 6:00 a.m. when I woke up. Instantly, I went into her bedroom to see if she was all right.

"Hi Doll," she said in a feeble voice. She frequently used that special endearment for me.

"How are you this morning, Mom?" I asked.

"I have a terrible headache. Do you think you could give me some medication for the pain?"

I knew the pain was caused by the cytomegalovirus. It was a relentless, agonizing pain that affected her daily. Dad was always reluctant to give her a full dose of over-the-counter pain medication. He was concerned she would become addicted to pain killers. One day I was so frustrated and angry, I exclaimed, "Dad, it doesn't make any difference. Mom won't live long enough to worry about being addicted to pain medication. She has pain in her head and all through her body. We can at least try to alleviate some of her pain." He shook his head and refused to give her more than one pain pill every four to six hours. Tonight, I refused to comply with his conservative approach of limiting her pain medication. Instead, I gave Mom the recommended adult dose. I was in charge now. Mom being addicted to a mild pain medication was the least of my concerns.

"Why don't you let me rub your head for a few minutes? It might help ease the pain," I offered.

"I'd like that. Thank you for being so nice to me," she said, gratefully. She closed her eyes. I rubbed her forehead as I had done when I was a teenager. Mom was prone to tension headaches. However, this headache was different and was concentrated on one side of her head. Nothing seemed to ease her agonizing, intense pain.

After resting for a half hour, I carefully helped her to the bathroom. I couldn't let her fall two days before our trip to Florida. Not now…not after all this effort.

At breakfast, she just stared at me as I cooked. I noticed her pill bag on the counter. She needed to take her medication after eating. I realized that I had to hide it from her in case she was confused and started taking some of the medication herself. A few weeks ago she was in charge of managing her own prescribed medications. Now that the dementia was affecting her cognitive abilities, I couldn't trust her to take the right medication at the appropriate times.

"Here you are, Mom." I placed a hard-boiled egg, two pieces of toast and orange juice in front of her.

"Do I smell some coffee brewing?" she asked.

"Yes, Mom, I have some coffee for you too. Sugar and cream?" I asked. She nodded and smiled at me to indicate her appreciation.

"This smells so good. Thank you so much for making me such a delicious breakfast, Nancy." I was so gratified to have provided this small pleasure in her life.

After she finished, I sorted out her pills for the morning. There were eight different pills…all different shapes and colors. As I set them down on the kitchen table, one pill accidentally rolled off the table onto the floor.

"I'll give you another pill, Mom. That one is dirty," I said.

She replied sadly, "It doesn't matter, Nancy. I'm already dirty."

It crushed me to hear her say those words. She saw herself as being so contaminated that she didn't deserve a clean pill. Society had instilled in her a sense of shame. It hurt me so much to have her perceive herself in that way. It wasn't fair that this wretched virus could cause so much emotional and physical pain to such a wonderful lady. No one should have to suffer with this horrific disease and feel the stigma attached to AIDS.

That afternoon, Mom decided to take a nap. I went into the kitchen and looked in the refrigerator for something for dinner. *Darn, I had forgotten to take the chicken out of the freezer for dinner.* Realizing we had nothing for supper, I thought I could walk over to the restaurant that was down the street and pick out something for us to eat. Freezing rain had been pelting down all day.

"Mom, I'm going to Fishland to get some dinner for us. Would you like some baked haddock?" I asked.

"Oh yes, you know how much I love haddock, Nancy," she replied with a grin on her face. "But please be careful. It looks slippery out there."

"Don't worry. I'll be just fine. It shouldn't take that long. Listen carefully…I don't want you to get out of bed while I'm gone. Do you understand? Just stay in bed," I said adamantly. Walking down the steps, I started to slip on the ice, but luckily caught my balance. I felt I was walking across a skating rink. I walked briskly but carefully and was able to get to the restaurant in about fifteen minutes. I ordered two haddock dinners and brought them home for our dinner. The thermometer outside the window registered 9 degrees Fahrenheit. Mom was sitting up in bed waiting anxiously for my return.

"We have a really tasty dinner tonight," I said excitedly. "I'll set up two trays and we can eat in the family room while we watch television."

"That will be nice. I want to watch *Highway to Heaven.*" This was one of Mom's favorite television shows. "After that, we can watch the news and weather."

A couple of hours after dinner, she said, "I think I'm going to bed early tonight. I didn't sleep well last night." I hoped she would sleep through the night and would not fall out of bed again.

Throughout the night, I could hear her moaning with pain. I went in her bedroom to give her some medication to relieve her relentless headache. An hour later she called on the intercom, "Nancy, I need you to help me go to the bathroom."

"Okay, Mom, I'm coming. Just don't get up until I get there."

After I helped her, she asked for a drink of cranberry juice that I brought to her. She slept the rest of the night. It was such a welcomed relief for me.

The following day I had four piano lessons scheduled in the afternoon. Floyd came down to stay with Mom while I went home to teach my students and make dinner for Tom and Shawn. While Floyd was taking care of Mom, she got up from her chair and tried to sneak the pill bag away from the couch where Floyd was sitting.

"No, you can't touch that, Mom," he said firmly. "Nancy would be very upset with me." Mom mumbled garbled words and sauntered back into her bedroom with a scowl on her face. The fact that she was not in control of most of her possessions anymore frustrated her.

After finishing my lessons and feeding Tom and Shawn dinner, I drove back to stay with Mom. As I entered the family room, I saw how distressed Floyd was. He hadn't been with her in a few days and was dismayed at the rapid decline in her health and mental status. He changed the sheets on her bed as she had another accident while she was sleeping. She was probably embarrassed to call him to have him help her to the bathroom.

Before Floyd left to go back home, he gave Mom and me a kiss good-night. "I'll pick you up tomorrow afternoon at one o'clock sharp. We have to get to the airport early to have your bags checked."

The rest of the evening I sat with Mom in the family room. It was so difficult to realize that tonight would probably be the last night she would be in her home. "At least I won't be as afraid to get some help cleaning the house in Florida," she said.

"Right now, I don't want anyone to find out about my HIV-infection, Nancy. I'm scared of what people might think of me. But after I'm gone, you'll have a last chapter for your book."

She was so proud of my magazine articles I had published about our family. She knew I was in the process of writing a book about the adversity we had gone through dealing with Shawn's cerebral palsy, Tom's dyslexia and my own medical conditions.

"I want you to write about me having AIDS because I don't want anyone else to suffer in silence like we have," she said. I didn't say anything. I nodded my head and held her hand.

We had a snack of tapioca pudding with a scoop of whipped cream on top before we went to bed. I hoped we would both sleep through the night. Tomorrow was going to be a very hectic day for both of us. As I helped Mom into bed, I kissed her on the forehead and said, "Sleep well, Mom. If you need me, just call or ring your bell and I will come right away."

"You're such a good daughter, Nancy. Thank you for helping me this week."

I thought to myself how wonderful she had been to me all these years. I tucked her into bed at ten o'clock and put her favorite music tape in the cassette player since it seemed to lull her to sleep. Appropriately, it was titled *Solace.*

I wasn't going to bed yet, and I would shut it off after she had fallen asleep. Walking into the family room, I noticed some interesting magazines. My mind was unable to focus on anything that required much concentration. About twenty-minutes later, I peeked in her bedroom. She was sound asleep. I shut off the music and went to bed. Tomorrow would be a long day. We both needed a good night's sleep for our plane trip.

~ 6 ~

Final Flight to Florida

Before leaving, I decided to give Mom a bath and style her hair. I wanted her to look pretty for Dad who would be meeting us at the West Palm Beach airport. While Mom was resting, I sat at the desk for a few minutes to catch my breath from cleaning and packing. As I was about to get up, the phone rang. It was my aunt calling from work.

"How are things going, Nancy?" she asked.

"Well, I'm just about ready to give Mom a bath."

"How are you going to manage that?"

As I sat in the chair, trying to gain strength, I responded, "I honestly haven't figured that out yet...but I will find a way. I have to hurry because Floyd will be coming here soon to take us to the airport."

Weak myself, I felt helping Mom in the shower would be dangerous to both of us. I wasn't strong enough to support her weight if she stood in the shower. After considerable thought, I decided to give her a sponge bath.

That would be safer and easier. I had a small electric heater next to her chair so she wouldn't get chilled. After washing her hair, I wrapped it in a towel and proceeded to carefully bathe her.

"Ouch, Nancy, that hurts!" Mom yelled. I knew her body was wracked with pain, so I had to be careful touching her. For protection in case she fell and started to bleed, I wore rubber gloves. I had a few cuts on my dry hands from the cold, dry weather. Even though I wasn't that worried, I still took safety precautions. After all, I did have my husband and two sons to consider.

After I finished bathing her, I helped Mom to the bed and began putting a diaper shield on her for protection. I knew it would be a long flight. I just couldn't take the chance of her having an accident on the plane. She balked at this and fought me as I attempted to put it on her.

"Nancy, I don't want to wear this," she complained.

"Yes, Mom, I know it's probably uncomfortable, but many women my age wear them for protection." She finally agreed. It was difficult pulling her sweat pants over her waist due to the large diaper.

Sweat poured down my forehead. My heart was beating through my chest.

"I have to take a shower now, Mom."

All the energy required to get Mom bathed and dressed exhausted me. I felt weak and lightheaded. I wasn't sure whether I could trust her to stay in bed while I was in the shower. *What if she fell and injured herself?* We were so close to leaving for Florida, I didn't want any accidents to happen now.

"Listen carefully, Mom. I need to take a shower now but you must stay in bed and not get up. I don't want you falling. Can you promise that?"

She nodded and said, "Yes, Nancy, I promise."

As I walked out of her bedroom, I heard her mumbling about the diaper I had put on her. I knew she was very angry at me as she kept tugging at it.

I jumped in the shower, and as I was washing my hair, I heard a crash from her bedroom. I dashed out of the shower with a small towel covering me and shampoo in my hair. Expecting to see her fallen on the floor, I was surprised to see her on the bed just as I had left her.

"Good girl, Mom. Just a few more minutes and I'll be finished. Just don't get up!" The noise I'd heard was only a piece of luggage that had fallen off her bed.

Finally, I finished my shower and peeked into her room. She hadn't moved. Trying to catch my breath, I rushed to get dressed before Floyd arrived to take us to the airport. After I was dressed, I helped Mom to her rocking chair in the family room. I had brought a video tape of an old Judy Garland show for us to watch while I was working on Mom's hair. Ever since I was in high school, I had always enjoyed Judy's singing. She sang with such passion. When I heard Judy sing, *Smile,* I felt a sense of peace flow through my body. The words were so appropriate to the difficult situation we were dealing with now. Listening to the music was relaxing, and relieved some of the anxiety I was experiencing. I remembered when Mom, Dad, and I went to see Judy Garland perform on the Boston Commons. Even though I was in college, Dad lifted me on his shoulders so I could get a better view of Judy singing. Mom was so afraid there would be a riot on the Boston Commons with over 100,000 people attending. But it was uneventful, and we all enjoyed the concert without having to worry about riots. Dad still talks about that night.

I proceeded to place rollers in Mom's hair so she would look attractive for Dad. I used a blow dryer since we didn't have time to let it dry naturally.

After her hair was fairly dry, I took out the rollers and began styling it for her. She was so appreciative of what I was doing for her.

Finally, her hair was done and she looked so beautiful with her new red jersey and black slacks. I wanted to dress her so she would be comfortable for the four hour flight.

I helped her to the lounge chair so she could watch television while I went into the kitchen to wash dishes and clean up. I picked up my suitcases in my bedroom and brought them to the front door. We would be leaving soon.

A few minutes later, Floyd arrived at the house to take us to Boston. Before we left the house, Mom held Floyd's arm and went through each room as if she were inspecting everything, making sure her house was in order. It was as if she knew she would never be returning to her house again. It was so heart-wrenching to see her going from room to room, arranging items so they would look perfect. It was important for her to leave a neat house.

While Floyd was walking her through the house, I realized I hadn't had time to eat breakfast. Mom had managed to eat an English muffin this morning along with her cup of coffee. Realizing we might not have a meal on the plane, I made myself a ham and cheese sandwich, but I couldn't eat more than three bites. I was so tense that even swallowing was difficult. Yet, I couldn't let these feelings show. I didn't want to upset Mom and cause her to worry about me.

Floyd brought the suitcases to the car. I went back to the house to make sure I had locked the front door. Mom sat in the back seat of the car and started joking with Floyd. "Are you sure you know the way to the airport, Draper?" she asked with a giggle.

"I sure do, and I'll get you there right on time," he assured her.

I could see Floyd's eyes well up with emotion. He knew Mom wouldn't live much longer. He tried his best to keep up a good conversation with her on our way to Boston. I was dog-tired and didn't add much to the jesting they seemed to enjoy.

After an hour ride into Boston, we arrived at the airport in plenty of time. Floyd stopped at the Delta terminal and helped Mom get into her wheelchair which she was bringing with her. Mom and I went inside to check the flight schedule. Floyd parked the car. By the time I had checked the schedule, Floyd was walking toward us.

"I can't believe it! Our flight has been delayed for five hours!" I exclaimed to Floyd. I pulled him aside. "I don't know if Mom can even handle an hour."

Well, since there wasn't much we could do, I opted for getting a sandwich and drink. "Do you want something to eat Mom?" I asked

"No, Nancy, I'm not really hungry."

I ordered a tuna sandwich with chips. I managed to eat a few bites, but then stopped. I just didn't have an appetite.

Mom starting picking at my potato chips. Noticing her eyeing my tuna sandwich, I asked, "Would you like the other half of my sandwich, Mom?"

She smiled and took the sandwich off my plate and ate it and the potato chips with obvious delight. *At least she won't be hungry on the plane,* I thought to myself as I winked at Floyd.

After we left the restaurant, Mom wanted to use the bathroom. I was prepared for situations like this. I wheeled her into the handicapped bathroom and helped her with the diaper shield. She still was complaining about it, but I wasn't about to take it off. There was no arguing in this matter. In a few hours she would be meeting Dad and her friends in Florida. I couldn't take a chance on her having an accident since I didn't have an extra pair of pants. The bag I was carrying was filled with books, latex gloves, diaper shields, and cough drops in case she had a coughing spell on the plane.

Since Mom looked so pretty, I asked Floyd to take a picture of us before he left. I suspected that this might be the last good picture of Mom.

"That's a nice smile, Mom," Floyd exclaimed.

"Thank you for bringing us to the airport today, Floyd," she said. "I'll see you later. Drive safely."

After kissing Mom on the cheek, he gave me a big kiss and hug and said, "I guess it's time for me to go now. Tom and Shawn will be coming home from school soon."

Before leaving, Floyd pulled me aside. "Will you be okay with Mom now?" he asked as he held my hand.

"We'll be fine," I assured him. "It's okay. Mom and I will find something to keep us busy until we board the plane."

I noticed a book store directly across from the restaurant. Mom was an avid reader and a frequent visitor to the public library. "How would you like to browse in the bookstore, Mom?" I asked.

"Yes, that would be fine, Nancy," she said softly. She appeared tired and her head began to droop down.

As I pushed her wheelchair around the store, I stopped to pick up some mystery books I thought she would enjoy.

"Does this look interesting to you, Mom?" She nodded her head as if it really didn't matter. I had three books on her lap and headed for the checkout counter. I knew I would read at least one of them. It was obvious she was tired from all this rushing and now waiting for the plane to take off. *Another three hours...how would we ever make it?*

After we bought the books, we went to the designated gate for departure. Mom sat in her wheelchair and I sat across from her. After a few minutes, Mom closed her eyes. She dozed off for almost an hour. It had been a long day for her so far and yet we still had several hours before we met Dad. My head was throbbing with pain. I took a couple of aspirin for relief.

Her eyes opened when she heard the announcement, "Flight number 714 to West Palm Beach is ready for boarding. Anyone requiring special assistance, please come to the gate at this time," the stewardess announced.

I pushed Mom to the gate and a stewardess wheeled Mom down the ramp onto the plane. Since her wheelchair was too wide to fit through the narrow aisle, the assistant helped her switch to a narrower wheelchair designed to go through airplane aisles.

"No, no, don't take my wheelchair!" she exclaimed emphatically as she held onto it. She was afraid someone would take it, and she wouldn't get it back.

"Your wheelchair will be safe," the male attendant assured her. "We'll put it in the front of the plane so when you get off in West Palm Beach, you'll have it." He spoke softly and said, "Please don't be concerned." She agreed and her worries subsided. She was now having difficulty talking coherently, and I could tell she was extremely tired from all this activity.

I was sweating from carrying and pushing her through the terminals. After twenty minutes into the flight, Mom started coughing. I fumbled through my pocketbook searching for the cough drops. My other bag was above our seats. Just as I was about to look in that bag, the man on the other

73

side of the aisle reached his hand toward Mom and said, "Here, this might help," as he smiled at her and offered her a cough drop.

She smiled back at the man and nodded in appreciation to his kind gesture. Mom used the head pillow the stewardess gave her and immediately put her head back and rested. I noticed the grimaces on her face as if she was in pain.

About an hour later, Mom woke and whispered, "Nancy, I have to go to the bathroom again. I'm sorry."

"That's fine, Mom, I'll help you."

I thought how small those airplane lavatories were and wondered how we could maneuver this. But I knew we *had* to find a way to get to the bathroom. I waved to the stewardess as she walked up the aisle attempting to get her attention. I knew I couldn't take Mom back there alone.

"Excuse me," I said, "Could I have your assistance in helping my mother down the aisle to the bathroom?"

She said, "Of course. But can you wait a few minutes?"

I replied, "Yes, I guess we can wait a little bit but she really does have to go, and I can't take her alone."

She came back quickly with an apology. "I'm sorry I couldn't get to you sooner."

We both tried to lift Mom from the seat but because she had no strength of her own, she felt like a dead weight. Finally, we did get her in the aisle. However, she was very unsteady on her feet and was falling to the side.

The stewardess whispered, "Is it cancer?"

I just nodded my head. I couldn't tell her in the middle of the aisle that my mother was dying of AIDS. We made it to the lavatory just in time. I had my latex gloves stuck in my pocket and a small diaper shield in my bag in case of an accident. I felt faint and my legs felt like jelly as I attempted to help Mom use the toilet. Thank goodness we were both small women. Otherwise, we never would have succeeded.

Mom managed to sleep the rest of the flight. My head continued to throb with pain. My eyes were burning with fatigue. I tried to watch the movie, but it was useless since my mind couldn't concentrate on anything but Mom. I was looking forward to meeting Dad at the airport so he could help me. I was emotionally and physically depleted.

"Please keep your seat belts on as we prepare to land in West Palm Beach," the flight captain announced.

A few minutes later, we landed and the stewardess told me to remain seated until everyone had departed the plane. "I'll bring you a wheelchair in a few minutes," she said to Mom.

Shortly after the passengers had departed, the stewardess helped Mom get into the narrower wheelchair to maneuver her through the aisle. Mom thanked her sweetly.

When we were out of the plane, the stewardess brought Mom's own wheelchair to her. How happy she was to get it back.

Dad greeted us at the gate and waved as he quickly walked over to us. He was delighted to see Mom. When he reached us, he gave Mom a hug and began talking to her. His joy soon turned to shock. Mom barely said a word to him. Dad couldn't believe how Mom's physical and neurological condition had deteriorated in just a week.

I felt guilty at the sense of relief I felt now that Dad was sharing the responsibility. I hadn't slept for more than two hours for the past four nights and my muscles and joints were aching. I longed to have someone to share my burden with. It was difficult dealing with the secrecy of Mom's illness.

I hated pretending that Mom was dying of cancer. I never said what type of cancer she was suffering from. Friends asked about chemotherapy, and I really didn't have any answers to their questions as she didn't receive any chemotherapy or radiation. I would respond with a nebulous answer that seemed to satisfy their curiosity.

Dad was with a family friend, Jim, who volunteered to take Dad to the airport to help bring Mom back to their Florida home. He was unaware that Mom had AIDS.

Fortunately, he was driving his new van so Mom was able to lie down in the back seat next to Dad who held Mom's hand for the hour ride to their house. She was moaning in relentless pain.

During our drive back to the house, Jim made a remark about AIDS as we passed a poor section of town. I had to keep my mouth closed, but I was so tempted to SCREAM, "My mother has AIDS! STOP, STOP!" I wasn't allowed to say anything. As my father had said, "This has to remain a secret." If Jim had known Mom was infected, he never would have made that remark. He had always cared deeply for my mother.

Finally, we arrived home and my father and Jim helped Mom inside the house. Dad had the house in perfect shape for Mom's arrival.

"I'm so tired," she said. "I want to go to bed."

I felt as if I were on the edge of a cliff ready to fall off. After Dad and I got Mom prepared for bed I said, "Dad I need to take a walk and get some fresh Florida air."

My poor father understood and said, "Thank you so much Nancy. Go and take some time for yourself."

He was so thankful and happy that I had brought Mom down to their Florida home. I walked down by the pool and sat in a lounge chair. I had always believed that God would not give us more than we could handle. However, this was a real test of faith. It was one of the darkest moments of my life. Instinctively, I knew her days were coming to an end, and she would not be returning to her beloved home. Now we would have to wait and see how her illness progressed. Hopefully, she would be spared the myriad of deadly opportunistic infections that could cause her more pain. We would just have to take one day at a time and place her in God's hands.

~ 7 ~

Hospice Love

It was mid-January. The warm breeze blowing in from the bedroom window felt refreshing on my face as I sat on the bed after a long, restless night. Looking out the window, I marveled at the beautiful palm trees decorating the front yard. It was such a welcome change from the freezing temperatures of New England. It had been a tiring trip for Mom and me last night. The five hour delay in the flight from Boston to West Palm Beach had exhausted both of us. As I walked into the kitchen, I heard Dad talking to Mom.

When I entered her bedroom, I saw her tiny, frail body lying listlessly between her floral pink sheets. She woke up confused and disoriented. She wasn't the mother I had loved for so many years. She was losing her memory, her ability to speak coherently, and her ability to walk. I was losing my mother to AIDS!

Like a child, she was clutching a stuffed animal that she treasured. *Certainly, this silent mascot would not reveal the family secret we had been concealing for the past three years.* Only a handful of family members knew Mom had become infected with HIV eight years ago. Now, instead of enjoying her retirement years, she was living a nightmare and close to death.

I gazed at her face, pale and sallow, but her large brown eyes stared deeply into mine. She whispered in a tired, worn voice, "Nancy, you're precious. I love you."

Trying to hold back my intense emotions so I wouldn't break down in front of her was burdensome. I felt lonely, scared, and desperate. I needed someone to hold me, support me, and understand what I was going through. Dad had demanded that we keep Mom's illness a secret. I was obeying my parents' wishes. I couldn't *rock the boat* and reveal this stifling secret that was causing me so much anxiety.

They were afraid of what had happened to Ryan White and other victims of AIDS who were discriminated against for having this virus. The newspapers ran stories about Ryan White, a teenage hemophiliac, from Kokomo, Indiana who contracted HIV through a transfusion. His home town responded with fear and hate. Since Ryan was one of the first heterosexuals to contract the disease, the press covered the story. At the end of the school year, it was reported that Ryan White was kicked out of school because he was infected with HIV.

My mother worried about her grandchildren. She thought other children at school would tease them if they knew their grandmother was infected with HIV. For two years my two teenage sons were not aware their grandmother was HIV-positive. Floyd and I constantly whispered when we discussed

Mom's condition. We told them she was dying of cancer, but the constant secrecy was straining our marriage. We were both suffering without any support. Since I didn't have anyone else to share my sorrow with, I depended on Floyd for consolation. However, he was hurting as much as I was.

After much discussion, we finally decided to stop the whispering and reveal to Tom and Shawn that their grandmother was infected with HIV. Even though they were shocked and deeply saddened, they seemed to handle it well. They had been educated about AIDS in their health class in school and were aware that it was a virus that could affect anyone. I felt a tremendous sense of relief after telling them. At least we didn't have to whisper anymore.

The first morning in Florida I heard a knock on the front door. Dad was sitting on the porch eating breakfast. I glanced out the window and realized it was one of Mom's neighbors. I couldn't let anyone see her in this condition. One minute she was talking coherently and the next minute she spoke with gibberish words. I reluctantly opened the front door to greet Mom's friend.

"Hi Nancy, it's so good to see you again. I brought a little something for lunch."

"Joan, thank you so much for the chicken soup. It smells delicious, but I'm afraid you can't see Mom right now because she's sleeping." I could see the disappointment on Joan's face. She seemed so eager to visit with my mother.

"Oh, don't worry about that," she responded politely. "I'll come back at a more convenient time."

I looked at my father who was relieved that I had been able to tactfully avert Joan from seeing Mom in this state. My poor father couldn't take much more. Up four to five times a night to help her to the bathroom and give her medication, he was totally exhausted. He had always stayed with her or had me take care of Mom. He didn't seek help from anyone else so he wouldn't have to tell them about her infection. Going back into the bedroom, I sat on the bed watching her drift in and out of sleep. My energy was drained. Yet, I was still trying to hold on.

For breakfast, I had cereal with peaches and a cup of tea. As I sat with him, I said, "Dad, I think we need to take Mom to see Dr. Marston this week. Why don't you call and see if we can schedule an appointment."

Nodding his head in agreement, he replied, "Nancy, you're right. Her condition has really deteriorated in the past few days. I couldn't believe the weakened state Mom was in when you wheeled her off the airplane. It was a shock."

He picked up the address book beside his chair and dialed Dr. Marston's office immediately. After explaining Mom's condition to the nurse, he looked relieved. "You mean Dr. Marston can see her tomorrow afternoon?" he asked with surprise. "Thank you so much. We'll be there at two o'clock."

Finally, we were going to get some help for Mom. She was already taking AZT, also called Retrovir. It was the first anti-HIV drug produced. This drug was intended to slow the replication of the virus.

She had used an inhaler with medication to prevent *Pneumocystis carinii* pneumonia (PCP), a lung disease caused by a fungus. Her last blood work showed a dangerously low T-cell count of 52 which would make her more susceptible to other opportunistic infections. A T-cell count under 200 would be an indication that her immune system had been gravely weakened. Since her T-cell count had dropped under 200, this indicated that she had full-blown AIDS. A normal T-cell count is approximately 1000. After living eight years with the virus, a person could have a T-cell count of 200 which is borderline to an AIDS diagnosis. Her constant fever fluctuated between 100 and 102 degrees. She was unsteady on her feet and needed help walking.

The next morning Dad and I got Mom showered and dressed to get ready to go to her doctor's appointment. I styled her hair and dressed her in a pretty rose-colored jersey and black slacks. She seemed happy she was going to see Dr. Marston again. Mom felt very comfortable with her.

When we arrived at the doctor's office, we sat in the waiting room until Mom's name was called. Dad and I waited impatiently while Mom was being examined. I felt restless and knew that the results of the examination would be ominous. Twenty minutes later, Dr. Marston came into the room and walked over to us.

"You can come into my office now. I'd like to talk to both of you," she said somberly.

Gently, she said, "I'm sorry, but Irene is dying. You must know she has full-blown AIDS since she has CMV. She's in the last stage of the disease. Her T-cell count is extremely low. It's time now for you and Nancy to attempt to make her last few weeks or days as comfortable as possible."

Dad sat shaken by the news. Even though he knew AIDS was fatal, it was difficult for him to accept the reality of her death. Tears trickled down his cheek as he pulled a handkerchief out of his pocket. It took him a few minutes to begin talking again.

"Have you thought of the possibility of having hospice care?" Dr. Marston inquired.

"I don't understand, Dr. Marston," Dad said sadly. "If Irene is so sick and dying then shouldn't she be in a hospital?"

"No, she doesn't have to be in a hospital at all," Dr. Marston explained calmly. "She can stay in her own home with the help of hospice workers."

I had already thought of the idea and suggested to Dad that it would be good to have other people helping us during this difficult time. He agreed that we would be needing assistance with Mom.

"Do you mind if I call the local hospice chapter from your office?" I asked. Since it was Friday afternoon, I wanted to contact them before the weekend.

"That's an excellent idea, Nancy," Dr. Marston replied. "You can use my secretary's phone."

Dr. Marston led us to the examining room where Mom had been waiting patiently in her wheelchair. I felt sad that we had left her alone for such a long time. Surely, she overheard our conversation. As we walked toward her, I choked up and attempted to console her, but discovered my voice was paralyzed from the intense emotion. I knew I had to gain control over my feelings. I didn't want her to realize how painful this was for me.

She looked so beautiful. Her hair was styled nicely and she appeared so childlike, with a pleasing smile on her face. She didn't want to cause us any pain or trouble. That smile melted my heart. She was dying. I was going to lose her soon. How could I make her days more tolerable? She was plagued with constant head pain. No medication seemed to relieve her suffering.

Dad wheeled Mom into the waiting room while I went into the secretary's office to call hospice. The woman I spoke with was very understanding of our desperate situation after I described Mom's condition.

"Actually, I could have two of our workers visit with you and your mother next Monday if that's convenient for you," she suggested.

"Monday would be wonderful," I responded.

I was grateful that someone from hospice would be coming so soon. Yet, I worried how we would manage through the weekend.

Before we left the doctor's office, the nurse instructed us in the care of an AIDS patient and when it was necessary to take extra precautions. It was so horrifying! I prayed I would have the strength to know what to do and say to Mom.

I walked into the main waiting room and noticed an older woman and her daughter sitting together. It was obvious that they had heard the instructions the nurse had given us. They stared at me when I entered the room. Mom was waiting patiently in her wheelchair. Dad was still dazed from Dr. Marston's prognosis.

As I attempted to maneuver Mom's wheelchair and all the packages and pamphlets I was carrying, I accidentally dropped the rubber gloves on the floor. The daughter, who was about my age, stooped down to pick them up. Our eyes met. "Here, you dropped these," she said as she placed her hand on my shoulder to offer her support and sympathy in the tragedy we were facing.

A tropical rainstorm poured down relentlessly as we drove back home. Suddenly, without any quivering in her voice, Mom asked, "Nancy, how long did Dr. Marston say I had?"

Saddened by her question and knowing there was no comforting answer, I stumbled over the words, "Mom, no one knows how long any of us has to live, but the doctor did notice that you were weaker." I felt I wasn't lying to her and I knew that in her heart she was aware that it wouldn't be much longer. I didn't feel she needed me to reinforce that fact now.

Mom was suffering in silence with AIDS and fearful if people discovered she had the virus they would reject her. She was trying to protect all of us by keeping it confidential. Initially, I believed that people would naturally support us if they found out about Mom's HIV infection. However, as I sat in the back seat while we drove home, I remembered the day I had lunch with my friend, Pam, who was a devout Christian. We had often attended church and social events together. The topic of AIDS being taught in the classroom came into our conversation. She didn't think facts about AIDS should be discussed in the public school system.

"I think AIDS is a subject that should be talked about at home and not in a school room setting," she said adamantly.

"But Pam, this is a health epidemic affecting all segments of society. Many adults are not aware of the correct facts about HIV and AIDS. It's important for the students to understand them," I responded. "It will hopefully eradicate the fear and stigma attached to this vicious virus. Pam, what if I had AIDS? Would you still be my friend?" I asked.

"I'm going to be honest with you, Nancy," she responded, leaning over the table as she looked straight into my eyes. "I'd call you on the phone and wish you well, but I wouldn't want to be with you or hug you. I'm sorry, but that's exactly how I feel." I remember putting my sandwich down and leaning back into the seat. With shock, I sighed in disbelief.

"Pam, you've been my closest friend for over twelve years. How could you possibly turn your back on me?" I asked, hurt and confused.

"I'm truly sorry, but I could only support you from a distance.

I wouldn't want to be near you. I guess I'm afraid I'd catch it from you."

"But the only way you could contract the virus would be through sex, blood products, or sharing needles. You cannot catch it from casual contact like hugging me," I explained.

I tried not to overreact for fear she would suspect I had AIDS or that someone I knew had the virus. After all, we had just been talking about my mother's illness that she thought was cancer. *If this is how my Christian friends react, then how would my parents' friends respond to her?*

Mom had read dreadful stories of rejection and discrimination in the newspapers. She was too old and sick to fight people who wouldn't understand. I knew some people would be supportive, yet there might be others who would turn against them. But she needed love and caring from friends and relatives who did not realize she had AIDS. It was a huge burden to carry without emotional support.

Dad seemed rather quiet during the drive home. I looked at Mom who just sat staring out the car window in silence.

Suddenly, Dad asked, "How would you girls like to eat dinner at Shoney's tonight?" Mom's face lit up since she enjoyed their buffet dinner.

"Sounds good to me, Dad!" I exclaimed. *A diversion from the stressful visit at the doctor's office might be good for all of us,* I thought. Besides, none of us had the energy to cook dinner that evening. He wheeled Mom into the restaurant and the waitress sat us at a cozy booth.

Mom didn't say much but simply stared around the restaurant. Dad wheeled her up to the buffet table and asked her what she wanted on her plate. Pointing to different foods, he asked, "Irene, would you like some of this?" Mom nodded her head, expressing a desire to eat almost everything Dad had mentioned. A few minutes later, she came back to the table with food piled high on her plate. I knew she could never eat it all but I didn't say anything. Dad was still in denial and didn't realize how sick she was. She managed to eat a few bites of salad and just stared at the remaining food on her plate.

"What a shame!" Dad exclaimed. "All that food going to waste." He didn't realize that Mom's condition would suppress her appetite. He also didn't want to face the reality that his wife was dying. He loved her so much.

Obviously, Mom was also upset about Dr. Marston's prognosis. She knew she didn't have much longer, but was trying to make it easier on us by not letting her emotions show. I barely ate my clam chowder and turkey sandwich. My stomach felt queasy and my head was throbbing. I worried about everything we would be facing in the next few weeks. It was almost impossible for me to take much more.

We left the restaurant, and Dad put Mom to bed when we arrived home. Mom slept most of Saturday. In the afternoon, I went down to the club pool hoping to bask in the Florida sunshine for a few hours. After listening to soothing music on my walkman for an hour, I took off my earphones and overheard a conversation between a group of women who appeared to be in their sixties and seventies. They were complaining about their mothers and the little things that annoyed them. I was only in my forties and knew that I would be losing my mother soon. *How lucky these women were.* I felt envious of them and angry that they didn't appreciate their mothers.

Sunday morning Dad went to church and I stayed home to take care of Mom. The pain in her head was intensifying. Rubbing her head and stroking her arms brought Mom some relief. She enjoyed being touched and was grateful that I showed my love for her. Her hand kept reaching out to touch me. Despite the fact she spoke with garbled, hesitant words, I still managed to understand what she was attempting to say to me.

"I don't understand, Nancy," she said haltingly. "When I was first diagnosed with HIV, the doctor back home said I could live for several years. Why am I so sick now?"

"You have lived with this virus for many years. You were infected in 1983 and not diagnosed until 1988. That's five years when you didn't realize that you were infected with HIV. Now it's 1991 and your immune system is doing its best to fight this horrific virus. But your T-cell count is dropping. That's why you're feeling weak and sick."

Her eyes welled up with tears. It was so sad seeing her lying there like a baby without any strength and feeling so *dirty.* Many people thought only *bad people* were infected with the HIV. Mom's reputation was so very important to her.

"What would people think if they knew I had AIDS, Nancy? What if I am contagious to them?" she asked.

"Listen carefully, Mom," I instructed. "As I told you before, you are not in any way contagious to people by casual contact. No one can catch AIDS from you by holding your hand, kissing you, hugging you or even drinking out of the same glass. So please don't let your pretty little head worry about that."

Mom constantly had a dreadful fear she would be contagious to people. It was a question she kept asking. No one seemed to be able to allay her concerns. Dr. Webster tried to convince her that she was not contagious, but Mom seemed to worry about it anyway.

She glanced up and reached out to me with a tear rolling down her cheek. I continued to assure her that she wasn't putting anyone in danger.

"It's okay to have your friends in Florida visit you. They are in no danger, Mom. Secondly, there was nothing you did on your own to contract this terrifying disease. You are a *first-class lady* and should not be ashamed of having AIDS. In fact, no one should be stigmatized for having this insidious disease."

Her hands held tightly to mine. She was frightened and lonely. I held her close to show my love for her. I brushed her hair from her face to gaze at her beautiful skin and brown eyes staring deeply into mine. Even though AIDS can cause one to look emaciated and gaunt, Mom showed no signs of that. She had lost some weight though. Her skin was soft and clear. No one would suspect that she was dying from AIDS.

Before I left to cook Sunday dinner, I noticed she needed a new diaper shield. I went to the bathroom closet to get a diaper. I put latex gloves on for protection. She was getting used to this procedure now and fortunately didn't fight it as much, although she still disliked wearing a diaper.

She is so brave, I thought.

Then with a disturbed look on her face, she said weakly, "I hope God isn't mad at me."

"What are you saying, Mom? How could God ever be mad at you?" I asked perplexed.

In her quivering voice, she answered, "Nancy, today is Sunday. I haven't been to church in the past few weeks."

"Listen Mom, you're not strong enough to sit through the hour service. God knows that," I said reassuringly. "He loves you and so do I."

Leaning over, I kissed her on the cheek. "You try to get some rest now," I said. Before I left her room, I gave her some medication to ease her head pain which seemed to be localized on one side of her head. Nothing seemed to alleviate the throbbing. I took two pills out of the bottle and again accidentally dropped one on the floor. Mom noticed that I had dropped the pill. As I leaned over to pick it up, she said, "I told you not to worry about the pill being dirty because it dropped on the floor. I already feel *dirty*."

How could she ever think of herself that way?

Society had made her feel ashamed of her illness. I felt bitter and angry. I wanted to shout out that anyone can contract AIDS. It was affecting people of all ages, gender, and occupation. Sons, daughters, mothers, fathers, grandfathers, grandmothers, aunts, uncles, nephews, nieces, babies, co-workers, teachers, nurses, accountants; not just people in the homosexual community as most everyone thought.

It was getting close to dinner and Dad would be coming home from church soon. I put the chicken in the oven with the potatoes and carrots. A few minutes later the doorbell rang. Looking out the side window, I saw it was Mom's childhood friend. I couldn't let him see Mom like this. But he knew we were home. I was about to open the door when I noticed my latex gloves on the floor. I had put them down by her bed after I had changed her diaper. Quickly, I shoved them under the console table before I opened the front door.

Whew, that was a close call, I thought.

I had to be aware of these signs that could cause people to wonder about Mom's illness. If they spotted the bleach and latex gloves, it wouldn't take too much to put the pieces together. We had not really labeled her condition other than stating that she had a form of cancer. Most people thought it was lymphoma.

Opening the door, I welcomed her friend and politely said, "It's so nice to see you again, Jim. I wish you could visit Mom but she's not feeling well today." I quickly brushed him away from the front door before Mom could ask who I was talking with.

"Well, just tell Irene that I brought this little stuffed animal for her," he said as he walked down the front steps.

What wonderful friends she has, I thought. I knew they would understand and support her if they discovered she had AIDS. Yet, I wasn't the one to make that decision. That announcement had to come from Mom and Dad.

Dad arrived home from church shortly after Jim left the house. My chicken was still cooking. Mom had been able to rest for an hour and then hobbled out of her bedroom. "Mom, I told you not to try to walk by yourself. I don't want you to fall," I said.

"I'm sorry, Nancy," she said. "I didn't want to bother you." She sat in her peach colored rocking chair by the breeze way. Her head kept drooping as if she were going to pass out. I had to hurry our dinner. We ate at the table and Mom just picked at her food as she had in the restaurant.

All through dinner I kept thinking about tomorrow morning when the people from hospice would be visiting to explain their program in detail to Dad and me. They would have papers for Mom to sign that would give them permission to provide care and support for her. I worried whether Mom would consent to having people other than Dad and me take care of her.

Later that evening, Dad and I sat drinking our nightly cup of decaffeinated tea. "Nancy, would you ask Mom to sign the hospice permission papers?" he asked. "I'm afraid if I broach the subject to Mom she'll reject the idea of having someone come into the house to help us."

"Yes, Dad, I understand. I'll try to persuade her that hospice workers will be helpful to all of us. I don't know what magical words to use to convince her but I'm sure I can come up with something."

The following morning two hospice workers arrived promptly at ten o'clock. They talked to Dad and me before meeting Mom. They began to explain their program.

Joan, the case manager, looked at Dad and me and began discussing how hospice workers would take care of Mom at home.

"We want both of you to understand that hospice can't take extraordinary measures to lengthen Irene's life. We can't use any type of life support system. Our job is to make the patient more comfortable and provide support to the family members."

Looking at my father and me, Joan said, "If Irene signs the consent form today, we can have a nurse out here tomorrow afternoon."

I knew it was time to go into Mom's bedroom and find the words to convince her that these women could assist all of us and certainly provide Dad some respite and nursing help. We walked into the bedroom together.

"Hi Mom. I'd like you to meet these nice ladies from hospice who are here to provide some assistance for you. They'll help clean and take care of you like Dad and I have been doing."

She stared at us with her wide open eyes. She knew what was happening. "But for them to visit us it is necessary for you to sign the permission form they brought," I explained in an upbeat tone. "Is that okay with you?"

Mom agreed without hesitation. Relieved, I gave the paper and pen to Mom for her signature. "Just sign the best you can but don't worry if it isn't that neat," I assured her. I noticed that her handwriting had deteriorated. I handed it to Joan for her approval.

"That's fine, Irene," Joan assured her after checking over the permission paper. Mom had signed the document which would allow hospice to be part of her life during her last weeks or days on this earth. Dad felt a sense of relief that finally he would have assistance taking care of Mom. He was exhausted from the constant care and secrecy.

"Someone will come for a few hours every other day," they told us as we stood beside Mom's bed. "Tomorrow afternoon you will meet your nurse, Betty, who will come almost every day to check on your medical condition and take care of your physical needs."

I felt a sense of overwhelming relief since I would be going back home to my family tomorrow morning. Dad wouldn't be able to take me to the airport. Instead, he had asked his close friends to drive me to West Palm Beach.

In addition to receiving medical and emotional support from hospice, Mom would be able to share her secret with another person. I hoped she would be able to talk about her fears and concerns with her nurse.

Tuesday morning, when I walked into Mom's bedroom, she was sprawled on the floor. "Hi Nancy," she said nonchalantly as if she were simply resting in bed. I stood over her for a few seconds just staring at her pitiful body, and realized she was so demented that she was lying contentedly on the floor. I went back to get help from Dad. Together we boosted her back into bed.

During breakfast, I tried to eat my cereal but the lump in my throat kept any food from passing down. Attempting to hold back my tears as Mom stared at me, I was barely able to sip my tea.

"I don't want you to fly home today," Mom uttered sadly. "I'll miss you, Nancy." Her head dropped to gaze at the floor.

"Mom, I promise I'll be back soon," I replied. She looked mournfully at me. I gave her a kiss on the cheek. She squeezed my hand and said, "Thank you, Nancy. I don't know what I would do without you."

I checked the kitchen clock and realized I had little time to take a shower and get dressed. When I finished, I went into Mom's bedroom and sat for thirty minutes as I stroked her head and talked to her. Her tired, brown eyes were focused on my face. Suddenly, she began sobbing. There were no words…just tears. I hugged her and said, "I love you, Mom. I'll be back in two or three weeks. You can count on that."

How thankful I was that the hospice nurse would be making her first visit this afternoon. Mom would need someone to comfort her since I was leaving. Knowing this might be the last time I saw and touched my mother was immensely difficult.

A few minutes later, I heard a car pull into the driveway. It was time for me to leave. *How can I do this without breaking down?* Dad opened the front door to greet the couple who would drive me to the airport. I went back into Mom's bedroom and kissed my beloved mother good-bye.

The couple were friends of my parents but were not aware of the nightmare we were experiencing. There was no way I could confide in them. Again, the secrecy was destroying me. It was a lonely two hour ride to West Palm Beach. I wept all the way to the airport with a silent burden hidden in my heart.

~ 8 ~

"It's Okay To Let Go"

As I was riding the escalator down to the luggage area, I spotted Floyd waiting for me. He had been so supportive during this devastating time. Although we had dealt with other medical issues in the past with Shawn and me, all of those surgeries and medical issues put together did not compare to the gravity of dealing with my mother dying of AIDS.

"It's so nice to have you back home. I know you must be exhausted," he said as he gave me a long embrace. "How was your flight?"

"It was an upsetting flight," I answered. "I couldn't stop thinking about Mom. To make matters worse, we had severe turbulence and we were not able to get out of our seats. The flight attendants were unable to serve us any food. We couldn't even go to the bathroom."

Holding his arm for support as we walked to pick up my suitcases, I said, "It was so difficult leaving Mom this afternoon. I left her with a sinking feeling in my stomach."

"I'm so sorry, Nancy. It must have been so sad to leave her."

Trying to cheer my spirits, he asked, "Would you like something to eat?"

"I guess so. I only ate a half bowl of cereal this morning. I didn't have much of an appetite before I left Mom. It was so heart-breaking to see her so helpless. I held her hand and kissed her on the forehead to say good-bye."

Driving down the highway, Floyd said, "Nancy, I know you're tired but if you like, we can grab a bite to eat at this Italian restaurant before we go home. You can sit, relax, and tell me about the past few days."

"I'd like that," I sighed. "I need to talk about it. There were so many people there, but I couldn't talk openly to any of them," I said sadly.

We sat at the table in a cozy corner and ordered a large cheese pizza. At least I was able to get some food down. Looking at Floyd, I said, "It hurt so much to see Mom drifting in and out of sleep." I explained to Floyd the many decisions that had to be made concerning the funeral arrangements and church service. Helping Dad be Mom's caretaker for the past few months had taken a toll on my health. I hadn't had a good night's sleep in several months.

Tom and Shawn were still up when we arrived home. "How's Grammy doing?" Tom asked.

I looked at both Tom and Shawn and replied, "I'm afraid she isn't doing very well." I didn't want to hold anything back from them. "I think she probably has a few more weeks to live…but we have hospice workers taking care of her now."

An unhappy expression covered their faces. They went to bed shortly after my return home. I stayed up looking for photographs of Mom to put on the collage that would be displayed by her closed coffin. It was after 3:00 a.m. when I finally crawled into bed.

The following afternoon I began my regular teaching schedule. I hadn't been able to see my piano students for the past two weeks. It was nice to be back home with my family and teaching again.

Memories of my mother driving me to piano lessons ran through my mind. We couldn't afford a piano when I first started taking lessons at the age of eight. However, close friends of my parents let us borrow their piano for several years. I always had the desire to play the piano. At the age of five, I played on a small piano we bought at a toy store.

I started my public performances at an early age. My mother used to turn my pages at the town hall for various functions. In high school and college, I accompanied the choir. During my first year of college, they drove two hours during a blinding snow storm to see me perform during the Christmas concert. My grandmother came with them. How happy I was to see them there to listen to me play.

Eventually, Mom showed an interest in playing the piano. One Christmas, I bought her a portable keyboard to play and taught her some simple songs. She enjoyed playing some easy familiar songs. The four days I took care of her before we came to Florida, I played some music on the keyboard for her. She loved to listen to me play; it seemed to soothe her frazzled nerves.

After I returned from Florida, I called Dad every other night to check on Mom's health status. Two weeks later when I called, I asked her some questions on the phone. There was no reply…except an occasional moan. She could barely talk. I knew her condition had deteriorated. After finishing my conversation with Dad, I made the decision to fly back down to Florida to be with Mom. There was no question in my mind that her days were limited. Before I left, I made sure that Shawn and Tom had clothes packed to drive down in case Mom died before I came back home.

The following morning I made reservations to fly back to Florida during the last week in February. Because it was spring break for college students, my choice of dates was limited. I promised Mom I would come back and be with her. She was so sad to see me leave. Also, I knew this would be the last visit to be with her. She was getting sicker each day.

My father asked Jim to pick me up at the airport. He drove me back to my parents' house. When I arrived at their home, it was late but she was waiting for me. I stood by her hospital bed that Dad had rented.

"I told you I'd be back, Mom," I said, trying to be strong, yet feeling so weak.

Encouraging my mother to speak, Dad said, "Irene, say hi to Nancy… she's come back to visit with us."

Instead of words, Mom had a fixed gaze on my face. Dementia and the cytomegalovirus had caused her to lose the ability to talk.

"That's okay, Mom. I know you're saying, 'Hi Nancy,' in your heart." I rested my hand on her chest. "You don't have to say anything. Just be. I'm here," I reassured her. That evening I read some poems to her. She kept reaching her hands into the air…almost as if she were trying to reach someone she could see. She had done that during my last visit with her. Betty said that with her experience in working with dying patients, reaching their hands out was very common. She said they were probably seeing a loved one who had passed on.

The following afternoon Dad called the priest at his church to come over to talk to us. The hospice chaplain was scheduled to come that day as well. By coincidence, he appeared at our house within ten minutes of Father Joe's arrival. Dad and I took turns talking to them. Father Joe gave communion to my mother and then talked to me for a half hour. He talked about how Kimberly Bergalis had been a parishioner in his church and how she had become an AIDS activist. My parents had seen Kimberly Bergalis in church one Sunday morning. The Centers for Disease Control told her she almost certainly was infected with HIV blood by a local dentist, Dr. David Acer, who was HIV-positive. After being diagnosed with HIV infection, Kimberly Bergalis worked as an AIDS activist fighting for mandatory testing of health care workers and patients. In December, 1991, Kimberly died at the young age of twenty-three.

Father Joe understood my frustration in keeping this a secret.

"Nancy, it might be best for you to share with someone. It's difficult to keep a secret like this inside for as long as you have."

After speaking to Father Joe, I walked out on the porch and released my deep pent-up emotions to the hospice chaplain. "I can see you're a crusader, Nancy. That's why it's been so difficult for you to hold this secret in for the past three years."

"Yes, there's so much I want to do in memory of my mother."

He knew I was a writer and had published stories about my son, Shawn, who was born with cerebral palsy and other stories pertaining to our family adversities.

"I need to share this hurtful secret with someone," I said desperately. "The only people I can share with are my husband and two teenage sons. I don't want to burden Tom and Shawn with Mom's illness. They're young teenagers. Floyd hears about my feelings all the time."

"You've been through a great deal in your own immediate family. Now caring for your mother and making plans for her death is damaging to your emotional and physical health. Listen Nancy, for your own well-being, I suggest you share this burden with those people who *you* need to tell and who will support you through this terrible tragedy. Go ahead and write about your mother's fight with AIDS. It will help others who are suffering with the same secret."

Father Joe and the hospice chaplain helped me put my feelings into perspective. They had empathy and understood how all this secrecy was adversely affecting me.

Dad and I talked after they left as we drank orange juice in the kitchen. After all that discussion, we both needed a boost of energy.

"Nancy, after Mom dies, I think it's best that you forget this ever happened."

I was shocked at Dad's comment. *How could I ever forget the nightmare we had been experiencing the past few years? Besides, I never wanted to forget the tragedy that happened to Mom. I wanted to keep her memory alive so that others could see that AIDS was affecting not only homosexuals, drug addicts, hemophiliacs, and Haitians as the media was reporting. It was even affecting grandmothers and babies.*

I think Dad said those words because he thought it would continue to hurt me if I dwelled on Mom's suffering. However, that isn't my nature. I needed to do something in my mother's memory. I didn't want to forget the tragedy we had been through. I wanted her memory to *live on* and hopefully touch the hearts of others who were experiencing the same nightmare of battling AIDS. I went into Mom's room after Dad and I had talked for a bit. She was sleeping. I just sat in the chair next to her, wanting to be as close as I could while she was still alive.

Dad came in to change Mom's sheets. She was moaning with pain. She looked at him…her eyes were fixated on his face with a downhearted expression. It was if she were saying, "Don't worry…it won't be much longer."

The next morning, I watched Betty, as she was washing and dressing Mom. "How are you, my sweetie?" she asked as she held my mother's hand. Mom managed to respond with a slight smile. I felt so grateful that Mom was receiving love from such a caring and compassionate person who knew she had AIDS. She was dying with love and dignity in her own home. Betty, Mom's beloved hospice nurse, looked at me and whispered, "Be careful what you say in front of her because hearing is the last to go."

She was my mother's angel. When Betty walked into the bedroom, she would look at Mom and say, "How's my precious love today?" She would give her a kiss on her cheek. Betty had her special way of making my mother smile and laugh. How lucky we were to have her give so much needed attention and affection to Mom.

At first, Mom was able to carry on conversations with Betty. She said my mother talked about me and how proud she was of my music and writing. However, as Mom's health declined, she would only use facial expressions. Mom never failed to display delight through a simple smile when Betty was in the room changing her bed sheets, washing her, or giving her any medication she required. Betty would sometimes just sit next to her and chat as she held her hand and kept her company for awhile.

After Betty left, I sat by Mom's bedside. She was totally bedridden and used a catheter since she was too weak and unstable to walk. As I looked down at Mom, I was so happy to be there to hold her hand and just be by her side.

Dad attempted to feed her some shredded wheat for breakfast that morning but Mom's mouth was shut tight. Her lips were pressed together with an incredible force. I didn't think she had enough strength to fight Dad's efforts to feed her. He had to pry her mouth open with his hand to spoon feed her. I kept thinking that Mom could easily choke on the food since she had trouble swallowing. She kept shaking her head as if to say, "No, I don't want to eat."

Later that day, Dad explained his situation to Joan, one of the hospice workers who had stopped by. "Listen to me carefully," she said. "If Irene is fighting the food you are trying to feed her then she is trying to tell you something. I would stop force feeding her. If she is hungry, she will let you know."

"How can we get Irene back home in two months when she's in this condition?" he asked.

I sat stunned by his remark. It was difficult for me to comprehend the fact that Dad actually thought Mom would be traveling back to Boston. It was quite obvious that she had a short time left. He was in a state of denial.

"I don't think you'll have to worry about getting Irene back home," Joan replied sadly. "The disease is making her weaker each day and without eating and her kidneys shutting down, she is very close to death."

Dad's face registered total shock. "You mean she won't be able to fly back home?" he asked as he started to shed tears.

"Irene has full-blown AIDS, and she couldn't survive the trip," Joan explained. "I think you and Nancy should start planning her funeral arrangements now." She recommended a funeral parlor in a neighboring town that family members of her clients had used.

Before supper, my father went out to do some errands. I was alone with Mom. I leaned over her hospital bed with tears trickling down my face and whispered, "Mom, I know you can probably see things I can't. There's a beautiful place waiting for you. I want you to know that it's okay to let go whenever you're ready. Please… don't worry about me. I'll be all right. I'll miss you, but I promise I'll be okay. You've been a wonderful mother and I love you very much.

Whenever you're ready, Mom, go toward the light."

My voice was trembling with emotion, but I needed to tell her how I felt. Her chest heaved with a release of emotion. Her hand was entwined in mine. I didn't have much time left to hold her and to touch her. I would be flying home tomorrow night. I thanked God for this time with her.

The following afternoon, Dad called hospice to have a worker come over to stay with Mom while we went to plan the funeral arrangements. We knew it was just a matter of time before she would depart this life. We drove to the funeral parlor and spoke to the director who helped us plan Mom's wake and funeral.

Looking at my father, he asked, "Where do you live?"

My father told him his address and the man replied, "I live about six houses away from you."

Dad appeared nervous. He thought that the man would tell someone in the neighborhood.

He voiced his concerns to the director.

"I want you both to be assured that anything we discuss here at the funeral home is strictly confidential. So you have nothing to be worried about."

Dad seemed somewhat relieved by that reassurance. He continued to talk to the director about what he would like for Mom's service.

"Because Irene has AIDS, we thought it would be best to have her cremated and have her ashes sent back home to Massachusetts. Then we wouldn't be required to reveal the cause of her death when we send her ashes to the funeral parlor," he explained. "I don't want the funeral director to know that Irene died of AIDS. He's a friend of ours."

"I have a suggestion for you. You could have an open casket for the family viewing and then we would close it for the public. We wouldn't have to embalm her. You could purchase an urn for her ashes and send them back home."

Dad and I started looking at the numerous types of urns. He suddenly left to go into another room for a few minutes. I stood alone with the kind gentleman who was explaining all the features of the different urns. Looking at the selection of urns was dreadful.

Tears began to flood down my cheeks. I couldn't even speak. My guarded emotions had failed me. I wasn't as strong as I wanted to be. I thought of my mother home in bed all alone with the hospice volunteer, and here we were purchasing an urn for her ashes. I had lost the control I had been keeping in for so long.

The funeral director held me and said he understood how difficult this was for both Dad and me. A few minutes later, Dad came back into the room. I was able to get my emotions back in control just in time, although Dad noticed my red, teary eyes. We finally picked out an urn and a casket that we could rent for the wake at the funeral parlor.

I was planning a church service for Mom and wanted to choose some of her favorite songs. Since she was going to have a closed casket and not be viewed by her friends, I was still working on a photo collage of Mom to display by the casket. On the way home from the funeral home, I glanced at my watch.

"Dad, remember I have to catch a plane back home tonight. I'll have to leave in about five hours."

"Yes, Nancy, I know you have to go back home, but I'm trying not to think about it. I'll miss you. I don't know if I could have done all this alone."

It was difficult to decide whether to stay with Mom until she died or to go home and get everything ready for the funeral. We had no idea if she would last two weeks or two days. There was no way of determining that. I checked with the airlines and it was almost impossible to catch a flight out in a week or two. I decided to go home on my scheduled flight. I had said my final good-byes to Mom. There was a lot of work to be done at home to make everything run smoothly so no one would suspect she had died of AIDS.

I had about two hours to be alone with Mom. I put a tape in the cassette recorder and played the song, *The Wind Beneath My Wings*, sung by Bette Midler. I noticed Mom's breathing was becoming extremely labored. Her kidneys were shutting down. "Mom, this will always be our connecting song. Whenever I hear it, I'll know that you're sending me a message from Heaven." She opened her eyes slightly for a second as if she heard and understood what I had said to her.

Mom was on her way to another land… a land of peace and love and freedom from suffering. *How could I be selfish and wish her to linger on after this tragic battle?* I looked at her eyes, one half open, and the other closed. As I left her that night, I leaned over her hospital bed and said,

"Mom, remember how much I love you. We'll meet again in another place in another time. Remember, it's okay to let go."

I only had another half-hour to hold her hand and touch her. My flight was departing tonight at seven o'clock. The next time I would see Mom would probably be when she was in a casket. I wanted to memorize every facial feature, especially her sentimental brown eyes and her soft gentle hands. Her face was so clear and soft. She did not have the facial sores that many AIDS victims develop. No one would suspect she had AIDS.

I heard my parents' friends walk in the house. They were taking me to the airport again.

"I have to go now, Mom. Remember how much I love you. I kissed her on the forehead and then walked out of her bedroom knowing it would be the last time I would be with her. Leaving Mom was heart-wrenching and the most difficult thing I've ever had to do. I cried all the way to the West Palm Beach airport.

Four days later, I had a meeting at school on Friday morning March 8th about Tom's dyslexia and making accommodations for him. I notified the teachers and guidance staff that my mother was dying. I informed them that we would be taking Tom and Shawn out of school for about a week, for my mother's funeral.

That night I went to bed around midnight. The phone rang a few minutes later. It was 12:15 a.m.

"She's gone, Nancy," my father's voice cried. "She died in my arms a few minutes ago, but it was beautiful. I held her while she took her last few breaths. She's at peace now."

Those last few nights, Dad called Sally, one of my mother's hospice workers, to stay with Mom during the night so he could get some sleep. When

Sally noticed Mom's respiration becoming labored, she knew they were my mother's last breaths for her final minutes on this earth. She knocked on my father's bedroom door and told him that my mother was close to death. Dad went into her room and was with her as she passed on to a new life without pain, suffering, and secrecy.

After the phone call, I stayed in bed, relieved that it was all over. Mom was in safe hands and not suffering anymore. Floyd got up and went downstairs. He was distraught over Mom's passing. Sleep didn't come easily to me that night. I don't think I even shed a tear when Dad told me. I was still in the mode of keeping my feelings inside. I felt like a robot. I had plenty of practice not expressing emotion when someone mentioned AIDS.

The next morning when Tom and Shawn woke up, Floyd and I told them of their grandmother's death. It was Saturday morning so they didn't have to go to school. They were saddened that she had died battling a horrific and stigmatizing disease.

Sunday, the four of us would drive to Florida for the wake and funeral which would be held on Tuesday and Wednesday of the following week. The following morning I returned from Florida, I took a picture of Mom to a photo shop for framing. She was holding Shawn as a baby. I asked them to try to frame it as soon as possible, since my mother was close to death and we wanted to display it for the funeral. Fortunately, it was ready to be picked up that Saturday morning. We would be able to put it on her casket for the wake and funeral services. We packed the car that day and left on Sunday for Florida.

I had decided to stay with Dad for awhile after the funeral. I couldn't let him be alone. We both needed each other so much. Floyd and the boys would drive back home without me. They stayed with Dad and me until the end of the week, and then went back home on Saturday so they could return to school. Dad and I would be alone supporting and comforting each other in this difficult time of mourning and heartache.

~ 9 ~

When I Must Leave You

After I returned home from Florida, I found a poem that Helen Steiner Rice had written titled, *When I Must Leave You*. It was in a book Mom had given me before she went in the hospital for her heart bypass surgery. I felt these words would express Mom's feelings:

When I must leave you for a little while,

Please do not grieve and shed wild tears

And hug your sorrow to you through the years,

But start out bravely with a gallant smile;

And for my sake and in my name

Live on and do all things the same,

Feed not your loneliness on empty days

Reach out your hand in comfort and in cheer

And I in turn will comfort you and hold you near;

And never, never be afraid to die,

For I am waiting for you in the sky!

My friend, Bob, printed the poem on his computer. I found a frame that would give it the right touch. He delivered it to our house a couple of days before Mom's death. We planned to place it near her casket along with the photo collage.

I had already packed clothes for Shawn and Tom for traveling to Florida. Mine were all ready packed since I knew I would be staying with Dad after the service. It took us two days to drive to Florida. When we arrived at Dad's house, he was so delighted and relieved to see us. He had been mourning all alone. The whole ordeal had taken such a toll on him for the past three years. He had been such a loving husband to Mom from the moment she was tested for HIV in 1988 to her final days. She died at the age of sixty-nine, three years after her diagnosis.

Mom had always looked so attractive in the blue dress that Dad and I had picked out for her viewing. The night before the wake, he searched frantically for the ideal necklace to complement her dress, but was unable to locate one. He rummaged through her jewelry box to find one that would be appropriate. He was becoming so obsessed and upset when he couldn't locate the perfect necklace. I offered him one of my own which he gratefully accepted. It was a white beaded necklace that looked lovely with her dress.

Eventually, he calmed down and felt relieved that she would look pretty in the casket. We had planned to have it opened for the immediate family. Only a few family members who would be attending the wake and funeral were aware that Mom had been infected with HIV. The other relatives who were coming did not realize she died from AIDS. The secrecy was still continuing.

That night, other family members flew down to attend the services. At the wake, the immediate family members were able to view Mom in the casket. As we sat down for the wake service, the music in the background began to play one of her favorite songs, *On Eagle's Wings.* During the wake, a friend from her high school gave the eulogy. Everything went smoothly. Betty, Sally, and two other hospice workers came to offer their sympathy and support and to say their good-byes to Mom. They were like family to Dad and me.

The following day we went to the church for my mother's funeral. The funeral car was late in picking us up but we eventually got to the church on time. Mom always enjoyed the organist, and he certainly paid tribute to her by playing the songs I had chosen and singing them with such passion in his voice.

After the funeral mass, I watched Mom's casket being taken into the hearse. I stared at the car until it turned the corner out of my view. Mom's body was being taken to the crematorium. Floyd saw me staring at the hearse and gently held my arm to help me to the car that was waiting for us. Floyd, Tom, Shawn, and I were ushered into the funeral car that would take us to the clubhouse at their mobile home park where people in the community had planned a reception for the guests. The laughing and joking between family and friends was just too much for me to handle. I kept thinking of where my mother was being taken. I went into the bathroom and stayed inside the stall for several minutes crying. I just couldn't face dealing with people knowing what was happening to my mother. The people at the reception were lively and excited to see each other. The party atmosphere was too much for me to endure.

Finally, the friends and relatives went home. Floyd, Tom, and Shawn stayed with us a couple of days and then went back to New Hampshire. I had planned to stay a couple of weeks longer to be with my father. Dad and I passed the day going out together and talking. We tried to do things that would take our minds off the ordeal we had been through.

One afternoon Dad asked, "Nancy, how would you like to go on a one day cruise?"

"Dad, I would love that," I replied. "We sure could use some relaxation."

The following day we spent several hours on a cruise ship just enjoying hearty meals and relaxation. We also participated in the entertainment on the ship. Dad looked at me and asked, "Why don't you enter the hula hoop contest?"

I looked at the people around the room with hula hoops. I knew Dad needed some amusement. "Okay, Dad, I'll get out in the middle of the floor and try to keep the hula hoop going for as long as I can. But if I make a fool of myself, I don't want to hear you laughing," I joked with him. He was laughing and enjoying the merriment as he watched me attempt to keep the hula hoop rotating around my hips. At least I had taken his thoughts away from Mom for a short time. I managed to come in second place. I lost to a teenager, so I didn't feel so bad. Dad was so proud and amused. He laughed as I swung my hips around to keep the hula hoop in motion. On the way home, Dad couldn't stop talking about the fun we had together on the cruise ship.

It was late when we docked back in West Palm Beach. Since we had left early in the morning, I had accidentally left the car lights on. The battery in the car was dead. Fortunately, a kind gentleman offered to jump start Dad's car. I managed to drive us back home in a torrential rain storm.

Talking to neighbors and friends was difficult since we couldn't tell them what Mom had died from. We dodged a lot of questions. I felt there really was no reason to keep it a secret; especially after her death, but out of respect for my father I said nothing about my mother dying from complications from AIDS. Again, Dad mentioned that we should move on and try to forget what we had been through.

"Dad, I never will forget what Mom went through. And I don't want to forget about her." Since I was a writer, I knew I had to tell this story. I came home and wrote a short story using a pseudonym to protect Dad's privacy.

I desperately wanted to write a book, but Dad was terrified someone would discover our secret. I vacillated back and forth about writing the book and using my name. But I knew I had to use my real name since I planned to speak at functions and organizations.

I woke up early the morning I was to leave my father to go back to my own family. Dad was so sad that I was leaving him. We arrived at the airport and I went to the designated gate for departure to Boston. Since there were security measures being taken because of the Gulf War, my father couldn't accompany me to the gate. I remember Dad's face after we hugged and I walked toward my gate. He looked so helpless and lonely as I looked back to wave to him. We were both hurting so much.

Please Lord, give me someone to share this lonely secret with. A few minutes before our scheduled take off, I heard my name being called. I didn't know what was going on, but I wasn't about to let anyone give me a difficult time. I had already fought the battle of my life. I walked up to the counter and asked the stewardess, "Is there a problem?"

"Oh no, Mrs. Draper, we'd just like to know if you would mind changing your seat. You have a choice of sitting in the middle of the plane or the very last row. Do you mind?"

"Whew," I thought…"that was a close call." They only wanted me to change seats. I ended up picking the last seat in the plane. It was cramped but I wanted to be alone. I put my bags under the seat in front of me. A few minutes later, a petite woman came and sat next to me. We talked for a few minutes about where we could put our carry on luggage since there wasn't a great of room in the last two seats of the plane.

She asked, "Are you okay?" I guess she noticed my eyes were red from crying.

"Well, not really," I replied. "My mother just died two weeks ago. I've been staying with my father for the past two weeks."

She squeezed my hand. "I'm so sorry. I know what it's like to lose a loved one." Then she leaned over and whispered in my ear, "I just came back from San Francisco where I was taking care of my son's close friend from childhood. He was a psychologist. She hesitated for a minute and then said, "He died of AIDS."

Wow, Lord! That was a quick answer to my prayer. Yes, God had given me someone to share my burden with. I held back for a few seconds and then whispered in her ear, "My mother also died of AIDS." At first she didn't understand. It was incomprehensible for her that an older woman could have AIDS. I explained how she had contracted HIV blood from a blood transfusion.

She put her arms around me, and we started to cry. We both needed support and God somehow wanted my seat changed to sit in the last row with a person whom I could commiserate with. We talked and shared our stories.

Later, I put a pillow behind my head and put my earphones on to listen to my walkman. I just rested while listening to the music as I gazed at the clouds knowing Mom was now in a better place without pain or suffering. The music on my cassette played, *I can fly higher than an eagle, for you are the wind beneath my wings.*

When Floyd met me at the airport, I introduced him to the woman I had met. I was so fortunate to sit next to her on the way home and receive comfort from someone who understood first-hand what I had been through.

Two weeks later, I had an appointment with my doctor. First, his assistant examined me. I told her how I had just come back from my mother's funeral in Florida. My parents were also patients of this dermatologist. She consoled me and told me how harmful it was to my health to keep this secret inside for so many years. When Dr. Davis came into the examining room, he asked me how I was feeling. I told him what I had been going through during the past few years.

"Nancy, there shouldn't be any shame that your mother had AIDS. If you don't share your feelings with someone, your health will continue to decline. You have enough stress in your life," he cautioned. "I suggest you go home and call a close friend to reveal this secret you have been holding inside. It isn't fair to you to keep this to yourself all these years."

When I arrived home, I immediately called my friend, Joanne.

It was so nice to hear her voice on the other end of the telephone.

"Joanne, I really need to speak to you about something. Can you come over to my house this afternoon?"

"Of course, Nancy," she replied, her voice tinged with concern. "Is everything all right?"

"I'll tell you when you get here."

I prepared some tea and Joanne came over fifteen minutes later. We sat on the couch as I began to tell her my secret. "I just came back from an appointment with my doctor," I replied.

"Are you sick, Nancy?" she asked.

"No, Joanne, it's not about me. It's my mother who I wanted to talk about. My mother didn't die of cancer as I told you. She died of AIDS," I said, as I broke down in tears. "I'm sorry I didn't tell you sooner, but we were keeping it a secret. Mom received a blood transfusion during her heart bypass surgery in 1983," I explained, "and the blood was contaminated with HIV."

"Nancy, I'm so sorry," she said as she held me. I melted into her arms with relief.

"There shouldn't be any shame in her having been infected with HIV," she replied. "She was an unfortunate victim who was transfused with HIV contaminated blood."

"Thank you so much for being here. I wanted to tell you so often but I had promised my parents I would keep it a secret. I'm planning a memorial service for her in two weeks."

"I'll help you in anyway I can, Nancy," Joanne reassured me as she held my hand.

After we talked, I felt so relieved. Now I had someone to talk to about our family's battle with AIDS.

The following day I started preparing Mom's memorial service. I chose the same songs I had picked out for her funeral in Florida. Friends volunteered to make casseroles and desserts for the reception which made it easier on me.

At the service, it was difficult talking to people as they came through the receiving line. No one knew what Mom had died of except Joanne and our immediate family. I noticed a man coming through the receiving line that Mom had known for many years. She knew that his son had died of AIDS. The people in his community had given him a difficult time because his son was a homosexual, and had died of AIDS. How I wanted to talk to my mother's friend, but I couldn't say anything. Again, our secrecy was continuing.

Two weeks later, Dad asked me to look for a tombstone for Mom. I searched for a week for the perfect gravestone for her. Finally, on a rainy, Wednesday afternoon, that happened to be my 44th birthday, I purchased a tombstone that I thought Dad would like for Mom.

During the next two weeks, I was bursting with a need to express my feelings about what had happened. I wanted to help other people who were fighting the same battle. Finally, I began writing the story of Mom's battle with AIDS. I longed for the support from other people who were going through the loss of a loved one from AIDS.

~ 10 ~

Sewing the AIDS Panel

During church one Sunday morning, people were asking for prayers for their loved ones. I was stunned when I heard a man behind me announce, "Please pray for us. Our son just died of AIDS."

When I turned around to see who it was, I was shocked to find it was a couple we had been friendly with during Marriage Encounter twelve years ago. We hadn't seen them since that time. At the end of the service, I offered my sympathy to them. However, I couldn't divulge the fact that my mother also died of AIDS two months ago. I felt so restricted by this secret I was still carrying in my heart. The shame I felt at not offering more to this wonderful couple caused me to take action. I just couldn't go on this way anymore. Later that evening, I looked through some AIDS literature and found a support group in Lebanon, New Hampshire. I knew I had to share this secret with other people who were going through the same experience. I was determined for my own physical and mental health that I would contact the support group to find people who would understand what I was feeling. As the phone was ringing, I was formulating words I would say.

When someone answered, I dived right in. "Hi, my name is Nancy and I'm calling because I saw your support group listed in a booklet on AIDS. I desperately need someone to talk to right now."

"Well hello, Nancy, my name is Linda and I'm a member of the HIV/ AIDS support group here in Lebanon. If you need to talk, we're here to listen and help," she said in a soft, compassionate voice.

I told Linda the story of how we had kept my mother's illness a secret because my mother and father feared discrimination and rejection.

"Nancy, I know how you must be feeling. I lost my brother to AIDS a couple of years ago. There is still so much stigma associated with HIV/ AIDS. Let me offer you some suggestions that might help. There's something positive that you can do in memory of your mother," she said.

"I would love to keep my mother's memory alive. In fact, I'm in the process of writing a magazine story now," I responded.

"Well, have you heard of the AIDS Memorial Quilt that was started in San Francisco?" she inquired.

"No, I can't say I'm familiar with that, but can you tell me something about it?"

"Certainly," she replied. "The NAMES Project AIDS Memorial Quilt is a collection of panels in memory of someone who has died of AIDS. The panel is sewn to connect seven others to make a section of the Quilt. Each section contains eight panels. Sections of the Quilt travel throughout the world bringing awareness of AIDS to those who view this lasting memorial. When they are displayed, each segment is unfolded very carefully in respect to the individuals represented on the panels."

"How large is the panel?" I asked.

"It's the size of a human coffin which is 3-by-6-feet," she explained. "Don't worry, Nancy, I will send you instructions as to how to go about making the panel. In fact, if you finish it in time, you could bring it up to Dartmouth College in Hanover, New Hampshire where our support group will be hosting the NAMES Project AIDS Memorial Quilt Display on May 17, 18, and 19," she said. "I would also love to meet you there."

"What do I put on the panel?"

"Anything that would reflect your mother's life, such as her hobbies, interests and any message you would want to share with others throughout the world," she explained. "The Quilt will be traveling to hundreds of cities and towns in the United States, Canada and many different countries throughout Europe and other continents."

"Yes, I definitely want to design a panel for my mother. I'll work on it and have it completed by May 19th," I assured her. "My family and I will bring it to Dartmouth College to become part of the AIDS Quilt."

A couple of days later I received information and instructions in the mail on making the panel. Linda also included the history of the AIDS Memorial Quilt.

*It had started in San Francisco in June of 1987 when a small group of strangers gathered at a storefront to document the lives of friends they feared history could someday forget. These people wanted to create a living memorial for those who died from AIDS and thereby help people understand the devastating impact of this virus. This was the beginning of the foundation of the NAMES Project AIDS Memorial Quilt.

*The NAMES Project Foundation; Atlanta, Georgia.

In 1985, AIDS activist, Cleve Jones, created the idea of having a Quilt to commemorate a loved one lost to AIDS. When he was planning a candlelight march, he discovered that over 1,000 San Franciscans had died from AIDS. Jones asked the marchers to simply write a name of a loved one lost to AIDS on a poster or sheet. After the march, Cleve Jones and other marchers stood on ladders taping these placards on the San Francisco Federal Building. When the posters were on the building it appeared like a patchwork quilt. Two years later, Cleve Jones created the first official panel for the AIDS Memorial Quilt in memory of his friend, Marvin Feldman. In June, 1987, Jones and others joined together to formally organize the NAMES Project Foundation.

The rest of the nation caught on to this memorial very quickly. Panels representing the loss of loved ones from AIDS were sent to the San Francisco workshop. Volunteers sewed these panels together to form a 12-by-12 foot segment for the larger Quilt display. The Quilt was displayed for the first time on October 11, 1987 on the National Mall in Washington, D.C.

It included 1,920 panels and was larger than the size of a football field. That weekend, a staggering half million people visited the Quilt.

In October of 1988, the Quilt returned to Washington, D.C. with a total of 8,288 panels. They were displayed on the Ellipse in front of the White House. Those people attending included family members, friends, celebrities, politicians and lovers. These people participated in reading the names of the people represented on the Quilt panels. The following year the AIDS Quilt returned to the Ellipse in Washington, D.C. to continue to memorialize these loved ones who had died from AIDS. In 1989, when the Quilt was displayed once again in Washington, D.C. the number had increased to include 11,000 panels.

I was impressed with the history of the AIDS Memorial Quilt and had a passionate desire to design one in memory of my mother. After reading the directions carefully and not being an artist or seamstress like my mother, I wondered how I would accomplish this task. However, I sat down with pencil and paper and designed what I thought would reflect my mother's life.

A couple of days later, Joanne and I went to a local fabric shop to purchase material for the panel. Searching for the appropriate material for the panel, Joanne remarked, "Nancy, look at this pretty pattern and it's even on sale."

"Okay, let's get several feet of it. It will look nice as the border for the panel."

The sales woman kept asking me what I would be using the material for…obviously trying to be helpful. I concocted a story that I was making something for my daughter. How could I possibly tell her the material was going to be used in making an AIDS panel? She probably wouldn't even know what I was talking about. When we got the material and checked out at the cash register, the sales woman said, "That will be $65.90."

Joanne and I looked at each other in shock. Did we misread the price on the material? It was already cut for me so I couldn't tell them I didn't want so much. We laughed about the confusion when we were riding home that afternoon. We had arrived at the store twenty-five minutes before it closed, so we really didn't have time to determine how much material I would need to decorate the panel. The price really didn't matter. All I wanted was a panel that would keep my mother's memory alive. When I arrived home and started to check out the material, I realized there was enough to make five panels! Oh, well, I could always use the cloth for other things.

I designed a pattern on paper that would represent my mother's hobbies and personality. I also wanted to include a message that would be spread to people throughout the world to heighten the awareness of this tragic epidemic. Hopefully, the message would help eradicate the stigma associated with AIDS. Knowing how isolated and alone Mom felt, I wrote in the bottom corner of the panel the words, "It hurts to know you suffered in silence." The stigma and secrecy crushed Mom as much as the disease itself.

We had picked out a sturdy backing as Linda had suggested. I decided the best place to work on the panel would be on the living room floor where there would be more room. While Tom and Shawn were in school, pins, needles, thread, and pieces of material were scattered all over our living room. Since anyone could stop by, I had to be careful so no one would see what I was making.

One day, one of Tom's friends stopped by the house. Nervous that he would see what I was doing, I quickly picked up all the patterns and objects I had pinned on the panel. Of course, pins were still strewn all over the floor. Fortunately, he didn't suspect what I was doing.

Looking at my design on paper, I decided to begin by cutting the red material in the shape of a heart. I cut out felt material to make letters to write the words, "I MISS YOU," on the heart. The heart was placed in the middle of the panel. In the right hand corner, I sewed a palm tree to indicate how much she loved sitting under the Florida palm trees. To reflect her gardening skills, I placed flowers under the tree. Everything on the panel was then sewn by hand.

To personalize it, I drove to my mother's house and searched through her closet to see if I could use some material from her clothes. I found a skirt with a leaf design. I also used some material from one of her dresses. When I went in her kitchen, I spotted two of Mom's potholders. They'd be perfect to represent her love of cooking…especially her delicious chicken pot pie and the myriad of different desserts she made for family gatherings and holidays. In the bottom of the panel in a rectangular box, I wrote the words, "It hurts to know you suffered in silence."

My friend, Claire, volunteered to help me fasten down all the items I had sewn by hand. A heart with the words, "I MISS YOU," a palm tree, potholders, and flowers were fastened on the panel to ensure a safe journey across the cities in the United States and throughout every region in the world.

Finally, Claire eyed the panel carefully, and tired, but satisfied pronounced the panel ready to go to Dartmouth. "We did it!" she exclaimed.

"Thank you so much for sewing this together. I really appreciate your help and time," I said gratefully.

"It was my pleasure," she said, embracing me. I carried the bulky panel to my car as the full moon shone brightly. After arriving home, I put the final touches on this lasting memorial for Mom.

The next morning I laid it on the living room floor to take pictures. Then Floyd, Tom, and I carefully folded the panel and placed it in the back seat of Floyd's car. When we arrived at Dartmouth College, we noticed the auditorium was filled with hundreds of people viewing the Quilt display. Names of individuals on the panels were being called out over the loud speaker. The role call of names continued throughout the day…a litany of unsung heroes.

I spotted a worker dressed in a white uniform and inquired where I should bring my panel. She brought us over where my friend, Linda was busy checking in the new panels. We filled out forms and read everything carefully. We were promised anonymity. No one would know who designed my mother's panel and her name would not be mentioned. Confidentiality is sacred to the NAMES Project.

I put Floyd's P.O. Box for the address so we wouldn't be identified…still trying to keep the secret. At the closing of the display on Sunday afternoon, twenty-five new panels had been formally accepted into the AIDS Quilt to be included with the 15,000 that were already a part of the NAMES Project. One of the workers approached me and said, "Your mother is going to be traveling the world bringing a message to people to help end this stigma and discrimination." Finally, the photographer was ready to take a picture of the panel I had made in my mother's memory.

Linda asked, "Nancy, would you like to be in the picture?"

"No, I don't think so." I feared someone would discover the identity of my mother. Another worker asked me for the letter I had written to accompany the panel. I was still putting the finishing touches on my letter while I sat in the bleachers overlooking the Dartmouth gymnasium.

Floyd, Tom, Shawn, and I watched as they displayed my mother's panel on the wall. Approximately a thousand panels were displayed in the gymnasium that weekend. The entire Quilt at that time was comprised of 15,000 panels. It weighed twenty-nine tons and included thirty miles of stitching.

My mother's panel would be sewn together to seven other panels. A month later, it became part of a 12-by-12 foot segment. Linda sent me a picture of it. She was delighted as her brother's partner was also on the same section. She told me that over 8,700 visitors came to Hanover, New Hampshire that weekend to visit the NAMES Project AIDS Memorial Quilt.

A BURDEN OF SILENCE

We had the opportunity to see it a few months later in a town near Boston. I had requested it be sent there. My father was home from Florida and I wanted him to see it. He was touched to view her panel and appreciated all the effort I had put into making such a lasting memorial for Mom.

Avon Books contacted me shortly after the display to ask my permission to include my letter in a book titled, *A Promise to Remember: The NAMES Project Book of Letters* that was published in New York in 1992. I didn't use my name at the end of the letter to protect our privacy. The following message was in my letter:

The panel I made is a lasting memorial in memory of my mother who contracted AIDS through a blood transfusion. She suffered in silence because of the social stigma of AIDS.

Please don't make these victims embarrassed and ashamed of their illness, but reach out in love and embrace them.

When we begin to love, we can begin to heal one another.

My mother loved the ocean, palm trees and her beautiful flower garden. I have faith she is now in a gorgeous garden surrounded by the peace and love of God.

You were very brave, Mom, and it hurt me to see you suffer.

You were a wonderful mother who taught me so much about life.

I love you and I miss you, Mom.

I pray that people will become more compassionate and understanding of the tremendous hurt and loneliness these people and their families endure.

A loving daughter from New England

A few months later, I received another phone call from Linda saying that the quilt with my mother's panel was in Florence, Italy at the 1991 International AIDS Conference which numerous experts in AIDS were attending. Only 32 panels were on display at that conference. I felt honored that the panel I made in her memory was being displayed for such a prestigious group of doctors, dignitaries, and researchers.

By October of 1992, THE AIDS Memorial Quilt had increased in size and more names had been added. It included panels from all 50 states and 28 different countries. In 1996, the last display of the entire AIDS Memorial Quilt returned to Washington, D.C. and covered the entire National Mall. The Quilt continued to expand as the growing numbers of names of people lost to AIDS were added.

One day I read in our local newspaper that the NAMES Project AIDS Quilt was going to be displayed at our local high school. I called the Names Project in San Francisco and asked if my mother's section could be sent to our town. With only a week to go, they managed to get it there in time for the display. Three months before, I had confided to two of my close cousins that my mother had died of AIDS. They were very supportive and grateful to me that I had shared this long-held secret about their aunt.

How delighted I was to see them at the AIDS Quilt display at our school. My cousins and their husbands were standing over my mother's panel when Floyd and I walked in the room. They had never seen the AIDS Quilt display before and were deeply moved as they observed the decorations and read the messages on the many panels covering the auditorium floor. A teacher who was a close friend of mine was at the display also. I hoped she would have understood why I couldn't tell her the cause of my mother's death.

As I observed the display in the auditorium, I wondered how many more panels will be added to the Quilt before this pandemic ends. The Quilt segments that travel from city to city heightens awareness and educates people who had never known about this national memorial. As people walk by the panels on the floor or hanging on the walls, they see the face of a person who died from this disease.

Visiting the AIDS Memorial Quilt is a healing process for those of us who have been caretakers. As I look down at my mother's panel, memories begin to stir inside me. Thoughts of swimming in the ocean together, ice skating, fishing, family camping trips, attending concerts, wedding preparations, and sometimes giggling together in church or at a play when we were supposed to be somber. We had so much fun together. I miss those times. They are gone...but so is her suffering. Her memory will live on in the panel that educates and spreads the message of de-stigmatizing AIDS to thousands of people who view the Quilt. Hopefully, the stigma will be replaced with compassion and acceptance.

Today, in 2004, the Quilt includes 45,000 panels, weighs 54 tons, and represents 88,000 names of people who have died of AIDS. It has increased in size to cover over 30 football fields. According to the NAMES Project, it is 51.3 miles long if the 3-by-6 foot panels were laid end to end. Panels for Liberace, Arthur Ashe, Elizabeth Glaser, Rock Hudson, and Ryan White are displayed in the Quilt. In 1996, the NAMES Project moved the entire Quilt to a 14,000 square foot secure warehouse in Atlanta, Georgia.

A flower, heart, piano keys, trumpet, cat, sunset, sequins, red ribbon, picture, poem, and letter are some of the items that decorated the panels. Every panel is different and unique; but all pay tribute to loved ones lost to AIDS. The Quilt provides mounting evidence of the massive toll taken by this epidemic that is snuffing out the lives of millions of people throughout the entire world. At the end of 2003, 14 million people had visited the AIDS Memorial Quilt at various displays around the world. The NAMES Project AIDS Memorial Quilt was nominated for a Nobel Peace Prize in 1989. It is the largest ongoing community art project in the world. It has been displayed in auditoriums, schools, churches and on the National Mall in Washington, D.C.

When we brought the panel to Dartmouth College in Lebanon, New Hampshire, I watched Tom as he pushed Shawn's wheelchair around sections of the Quilt. They were teenagers and being educated about the dangers of AIDS. They were happy and proud that their grandmother's panel was going to be part of the larger Quilt.

Since they had learned a little about AIDS in their health class in high school, they were more knowledgeable about the dangers of HIV infection than many people. The AIDS Quilt could certainly be a positive aspect of any school's awareness program. Studies have indicated that school-based sex education programs have prevented the escalation of HIV infection. Knowledge is *life* and silence is *death* when dealing with such a vicious, but preventable disease.

As I left the gymnasium, I walked away with a feeling of peace in my heart knowing that I had made a lasting memorial for my mother. Her memory and message would continue to educate and bring awareness to those who are unaware of the nightmare of AIDS. Each name added is one more person who has died of AIDS. It could be a baby, brother, sister, mother, father, friend, or co-worker. The Quilt teaches compassion toward people infected with AIDS. It shows that this disease can happen to anyone.

A BURDEN OF SILENCE

AIDS doesn't discriminate, and we should not discriminate against people who have it. The panels sewn together tell stories of pain, rage, fear, courage, compassion, and love. Emotions stir within each individual who view the panels. The Quilt is given a moving and compassionate voice when the names are being called during each display. It plays such an important role in our country's education. The AIDS Quilt has the opportunity to touch souls. The Quilt can reach inside the hearts of people who view the many precious panels. Hopefully, people who visit the Quilt will listen to the voice behind each panel and hear the words…"Please, don't just walk by me. Please do something to end this disease. Please demand a cure. Please demand education to prevent further infection. Please don't judge, but reach out and embrace us with love and acceptance so the stigma and discrimination associated with AIDS will finally be eradicated. We are gone, but you can still do something to end this pandemic that is killing people every few seconds." On June 25-27, 2004, the NAMES Project displayed 8,000 new panels on the Ellipse in front of the White House. I had the honor of calling out some of the names that appeared on these new panels.

Hopefully, the AIDS Quilt will stir society to take action. Together, we can end this war against AIDS. Schools, churches, and various organizations can use the NAMES Project Memorial Quilt to help foster healing and promote education throughout our nation.

~ 11 ~

Speaking from the Heart

Several months after my mother died, I visited a friend in Michigan. When I was in the airport I looked for a place to sit while waiting for my flight to depart. I noticed there was an empty seat next to a woman with a Mary Kay bag beside her. I walked over and asked if anyone was sitting in the seat.

She smiled and responded, "No, I'm here by myself."

I commented on the bag by her feet. "I see you're a Mary Kay representative."

"Yes, I'm so excited. I just came back from the convention in Dallas." I noticed the name tag was still on her suit jacket.

"You must be Teri," I said. "Are you taking flight 455 into Boston?"

She nodded and said, "Oh, I forgot to take my name tag off. I was in such a rush to catch the plane," she laughed.

"I'm also a Mary Kay representative," I said excitedly.

Teri shared a little about the convention and then spoke of some of the troubles she had gone through during the past year. "It's been a difficult year for me," she said. "Last May, I lost my younger brother to AIDS."

Could this be happening twice? I had already met another lady on the plane in West Palm Beach who shared about her son's friend's death to AIDS. Now this woman was sharing about her brother's tragic death from AIDS. I believed God was answering me and placing people in my path to share my burden with. I leaned over and whispered, "I want you to know that a few months ago, my mother died of AIDS from a blood transfusion." She put her hand on my shoulder and then gave me a long embrace… two strangers bonded by a common tragedy became intimate within a few minutes. We shared our experiences until it was time to board the plane for Boston.

Before we parted, we shared addresses since we wanted to keep in touch. After we had been in the air for approximately twenty minutes, I began reading a book when Teri came over to ask if she could sit with me as there was an empty seat next to me.

"Of course," I said with delight. "We have so much to talk about."

During the flight home I shared with her how I had been vacillating about writing a book about my mother's battle with AIDS. I had already published two stories in inspirational magazines. However, I had used a pseudonym to protect our privacy.

Teri said, "Nancy, you said your mother wanted this story told. This is a subject that must not be shoved under the rug. It must be discussed and stories must be told about the isolation and fear people with HIV/AIDS experience. You must write this book to help others who are fighting the same battle as your mother and my brother did," she urged. "Someone has to begin shouting about this awful pandemic."

"You're right about that. I think you've convinced me. In fact, I've already made a panel for my mother for the AIDS Memorial Quilt."

"What's that?" she asked.

After I explained what the panels were and provided more information about the Quilt, Teri asked me to send her the instructions on making a panel for her brother. We were both helping each other.

For the next several months, we continued to keep in touch by mail. One night, Teri called me on the phone and said excitedly, "Nancy, I want you to know I made the panel for my brother Jack. I just found out that his panel will be on display in the Boston area next month. I'm so happy and thankful to you for informing me about the AIDS Quilt."

* * *

A couple of months later, Floyd and I were enjoying our meal at a wedding reception. Suddenly, a man sitting next to Floyd starting talking about AIDS. "Those people with AIDS deserve what they got. This is a curse from God. What if they are contagious?" He looked at Floyd and asked, "Would you want to be with someone with AIDS?"

Floyd looked at him and said, "I'd have no problem being with someone who has HIV or AIDS. Why should I? They're not contagious to anyone. Actually, we could be more contagious to them if we had a cold or virus."

I was proud of Floyd's response. But the man continued his rant. Anger stirred inside me. I couldn't sit there and listen to this conversation. It hurt me too much. The rage became so intense that I felt my heart would pound through my chest. I glanced down at my plate and abruptly put my fork and knife down on the table and went to the ladies' room. Not being able to respond was frustrating. After waiting inside the ladies' room for several minutes and using some deep breathing exercises, I was able to calm myself and return to the table.

Thankfully, the clod had left and was talking to people across the room. Hopefully, the panel I made would educate people like this man who was unaware that his son, daughter, nephew, niece, mother, father, or friend could contract AIDS. This virus could affect anyone who failed to use proper protection during sex, shared needles while using drugs or who had been infected with HIV through a blood transfusion. Most of the hemophiliacs who were treated with blood contaminated products before testing in March of 1985 died of AIDS. Thousands of young men and women who were already fighting their own battle with hemophilia died due to the negligence and lack of urgency in devising a test to determine if the blood they were receiving was HIV infected. Again, was it the cost of testing that resulted in such a delay of attacking this disease aggressively?

In February of 1991, *60 Minutes* ran a story on Red Cross blood. The segment featured transfusion-AIDS victims, including Roland Ray. Mr. Ray was transfused in 1984 due to a gunshot wound while working at a store outside of Washington, D.C. Judith Reitman, author of *Bad Blood,* writes that it was discovered that the Red Cross had learned in May, 1985 that Roland Ray's donor had tested positive for HIV. He had received this notification from the blood bank in 1989. It had taken four years before the Red Cross informed the hospital and Mr. Ray of the contaminated blood.

Meredith Vieira, a CBS News reporter, told *60 Minutes* viewers that a man named Roland Ray was one of the victims of the D.C. region who had, at least, been notified. "According to the FDA," Vieira reported, "Red Cross neglected to inform hundreds of people they might be infected with the

AIDS virus. A former Red Cross official told the FDA that tracking down victims is time consuming and expensive, and the Red Cross wanted to keep its budget down."

Hundreds and thousands of people like my mother who went into the hospital trusted doctors who assured patients that the blood was safe. So many lives were lost because of a lag in testing by blood banks throughout the United States.

Little did they know that eventually they might know someone with AIDS. AIDS is not a "dirty" four letter word that only affects homosexuals, intravenous drug users, hemophiliacs and Haitians. It doesn't discriminate between homosexual or heterosexual, wealthy or poor, Democrat or Republican, black or white, good or bad, young or old, or male or female.

Hopefully, this national memorial for AIDS will continue to foster healing and understanding to people throughout the world. It will send a WAKE UP call to people to end this war with awareness, education, and prevention. AIDS has been called by many experts one of the most preventable diseases the world has ever seen. It is also one of the worst mankind has seen. On December 1st of every year, World AIDS Day, heightens awareness about this heinous disease. Newscasters reported that in 2003, 8,000 people died of AIDS related diseases every day and 14,000 became infected daily worldwide. In the past two decades, since the pandemic began, 22 million people have died and 45 million have been infected. Every 14 seconds a young person under the age of twenty-five becomes infected. Women comprise fifty percent of all new infections according to the World AIDS Day report. In Africa, an AIDS victim is buried every 30 minutes. This must stop.

At the request of Congress, a study was conducted by the Institute of Medicine.* The study determined that "blood became a vector for HIV infection in the early and mid-1980's and caused more than half of the 16,000 hemophiliacs and over 12,000 blood transfusions recipients to contract AIDS."

The report stated that the Food and Drug Administration had been negligent and failed to protect the blood supply by not implementing screening options. These screening options were recommended by the Centers for Disease Control in 1983.

I feel that thousands of people like my mother were needlessly infected by the inept procedures taken by the FDA. *Was money more of a priority?* If measures had been taken to screen out those "high risk donors" then these precautionary actions according to the CDC would have eliminated thousands of HIV-contaminated blood to be transfused to recipients.

I was so happy that I had designed a panel for my mother for the NAMES Project Quilt. My mother's battle will not have been in vain if one person is touched by her panel. She fought a lonely battle by keeping her HIV/AIDS status a secret because she feared what people would think of her. Keeping her memory alive was important to me. Thankfully, I reached out for support and was led to design a panel that would commemorate her life through this living memorial.

With God's help, my mother's panel will reach the hearts of the millions of people who visit the AIDS Memorial Quilt each year. Someday, the

*see p.19, HIV and the Blood Supply: An Analysis of Crisis Decisionmaking, Institute of Medicine; National Academy Press, 1995.

stigma Mom feared most will be eradicated and replaced with love and compassion. We will become a better society because of it.

We will know the battle is over when no more panels have to be added to the AIDS Quilt. Until then, we must follow the advice of the World AIDS Day slogan for 2003-2004…"Live and let live," and reach out to those suffering with this ghastly disease that robs victims of their dignity and life.

With the help of hospices all over the world, AIDS victims and their families can receive the love, care, and compassion they so sorely need. My mother was blessed by the wonderful hospice workers who showered her with love. How thankful I am to them.

If Mom were here today, she would probably speak the following words:

"I'm sorry I didn't tell you that I had AIDS. I was scared of what you might think of me. I felt lonely and ashamed. Please forgive me for keeping this secret inside. It hurt me to do this. I didn't want to, but I feared you might reject me. Every day my heart ached with pain and anguish. Every day I felt like a leper. Every day I wept. I died an emotional death long before I died a physical death. I wish I could see all my grandchildren grow up and attend their graduations and weddings. But I will be watching from above. I will never leave you. If you meet someone who is infected with this tragic disease that killed me, please hold them and support them. They need to be touched, hugged, and accepted, not rejected. No one should have to suffer in silence because of AIDS. Reach out in compassion and you will be touching the heart of a human being that desperately needs your love, not rejection. Wipe the tears from their eyes. Hold them and embrace them.

They are not contagious, but in need of love and compassion. Listen to their words of fear and hold them near."

* * *

I pray that the message on the bottom of my mother's panel will touch the hearts of all those who view it as they read the words, "It hurts to know you suffered in silence."

I miss you, Mom.

About the Author

Nancy A. Draper has been writing inspirational stories for the past 23 years. She has been published in magazines in the United States, Canada, and Italy. After receiving her B.S. degree in Education from Keene State College, she taught elementary school for several years. For the past 24 years, she has taught piano to children and adults. She has spoken professionally about her stories, and how she overcame adversity in her life. Her hobbies and interests include playing piano, writing, holistic health, kayaking, yoga, and traveling throughout the United States and Europe. She and her husband enjoy summers at their Maine home, swimming, kayaking, and canoeing. Nancy and her husband live in New Hampshire. They have two adult sons.

Printed in the United States
20297LVS00006B/97-306